OUTCOME-BASED

EDUCATION

OUTCOME-BASED

OBE

EDUCATION

Understanding the Truth about Education Reform

RON SUNSERI

MULTNOMAH BOOKS · SISTERS OREGON

OUTCOME-BASED EDUCATION:
UNDERSTANDING THE TRUTH ABOUT EDUCATION REFORM

published by Multnomah Books
a part of the Questar publishing family

© 1994 by Ron Sunseri

International Standard Book Number: 0-88070-710-0

Printed in the United States of America

For information:
QUESTAR PUBLISHERS, INC.
POST OFFICE BOX 1720
SISTERS, OREGON 97759

94 95 96 97 98 99 00 01 02 — 10 9 8 7 6 5 4 3 2 1

Contents

Introduction

What becomes of the minds of today's students is the fabric of tomorrow's society. Education of children is the most important function a society engages in. Within those fertile minds are the seeds of its flowering or destruction. Because of its seminal influence on our nation, education and education reform involve every American. It is a discussion about who we are as a people and forebodingly, what we are fast becoming.

It is no secret that America is in dire need of educational reform. Comparatively speaking, the achievement levels of our students are a national disgrace. On this point at least there is unity. Something must be done. This is why, in 1991 as a state legislator in Oregon, I was encouraged to learn that an education reform bill was about to be introduced. Exciting things were happening in Oregon.

Not long after the bill was introduced, Ira Magaziner, then a member of the Carnegie Foundation's National Center on Education and the Economy (currently part of the Clinton Health Plan team), flew to Oregon to address a voluntary joint session of the House and Senate where he enthusiastically said, "All eyes are on Oregon. You are leading the way to education reform in this country." To have someone from the federal level come to Oregon and tell us that we were on the leading edge of education reform was very flattering. Few questions were asked and we didn't evaluate carefully what was said.

Because American education is in need of reform I was very hopeful when these changes were being discussed. At the time I knew very little about outcome-based education (OBE), as the new method of education in the bill was called. Therefore, I set out to learn as much as I could in the short time we had available. It soon became apparent that House Bill 3565, the *Outcome-Based Education bill,* called for changes so extreme that I instructed my staff to stop research on all other bills and focus on the content of H.B. 3565. What we uncovered gave rise to grave concerns.

The first truth that we discovered was that Mr. Magaziner had not been altogether straightforward with us. In no sense was Oregon "on the cutting edge of education reform in this country" with the implementation of OBE. Numerous states had experimented with OBE years before Oregon. There was no substance to Ira Magaziner's speech. It was pure hype.

We needed to learn the facts. My staff contacted every state in the country where any form of OBE had been implemented to see if an example of increased academic scores as a result of OBE could be found. There were none! That's right, not one. Scores had either gone down dramatically or, in a few cases, remained flat.

We learned that in Chicago, from the '70s through the early '80s, this form of education was implemented under the name Mastery Learning—same program, different name. What was the effect of OBE in Chicago? It was an unmitigated disaster. Almost 50 percent of the 39,000 students who began the program failed to graduate.[1] For those who did graduate, only one third were able to read at or above the national twelfth-grade level. Even more revealing was the fact that the teachers within the system didn't want their own children to be subjected to OBE. Forty-four percent of them sent their children to private schools.

Chicago School District soon became known as one of the very worst in the entire country. OBE was completely abandoned by 1982—many millions of taxpayer dollars later—but not before it caused political scandal. Parents, enraged at the education fiasco their children were forced to be a part of (a fiasco that damaged the futures of so many thousands of students), filed a lawsuit for educational malpractice. Finally the school district admitted the children had fallen behind considerably in their test scores.

Chicago is not alone in its academic results from OBE. The educational dysfunction experienced there has been repeated in each location OBE has been implemented. OBE has been thrown out of school districts in Colorado, Texas, and the entire state of Virginia, to name only a few. I was incredulous that certain politicians in Oregon were so thoroughly committed to the implementation of OBE when stories like Chicago's surfaced everywhere we looked. Most politicians who voted on this bill, however, didn't have any idea of its contents or implications. OBE has shown itself to be a system of education that:

1. De-emphasizes academics and focuses on changing behavior, attitudes, and feelings.
2. Holds top achievers back from further learning by making them teach the slower students.
3. Performs psychological tests on your children.
4. Keeps your children from graduating if they disagree with the values taught in school.

5. Forces fifteen- and sixteen-year-old students to make career decisions.
6. Is astronomically expensive.

In view of OBE's history, I was shocked at the lack of deliberation among Oregon legislators regarding the merits of this massive change. Even though Ira Magaziner seemingly chose not to be accurate in telling the Oregon legislature that we were leading the way in education reform, it was an effective, smooth political tactic. With the good will of the national education establishment, Oregon's OBE bill passed out of the House with only five dissenting votes, one of which was my own. Seven days before the end of the session, the bill passed out of the Senate. It became law almost immediately in July 1991 because of an attached "emergency" clause. As calculated by the bill's supporters, this move prevented a referral to the people for analysis and a vote. Every student in every grade in every public school in every district of the state must now be taught, according to the law, using Outcome-Based Education.

Don't be fooled into thinking that it couldn't happen in your state. It is happening everywhere. If OBE isn't in your district now, it will be in only a matter of time. If the federal government has its way, OBE will be the mode of education in every school in every state.

But don't despair. This book is designed to give you the information you need to stand up for what you believe education should accomplish in your school district. Remember, what becomes of the minds of today's students is the fabric of tomorrow's society. This debate is worthy of your greatest energies.

1. Alina Tugend, "Half of Chicago Students Drop Out, Study Finds: Problem Called Enormous 'Human Tragedy,'" *Education Week*, 6 March 1985.

CHAPTER ONE

Outcome-Based Education Explained

T he father of outcome-based education, William Spady, defines OBE as a means of "focusing and organizing all of the schools' programs and instructional efforts around clearly defined outcomes we want all students to demonstrate when they leave school.[1]

There is, however, far more to OBE than this isolated, innocuous definition from Spady. Who could find fault with such a modus operandi? It is suggested that this definition is packaged for maximum acceptance with minimum evaluation. A great deal has been written about OBE by its proponents to facilitate acceptance by parents and local teachers. Dr. Spady, director of the International Center on Outcome-Based Restructuring, is credited with having coined the phrase *outcome-based education*. It is very important to remember that Spady is not an educator. He is a sociologist. Education is the forum he has chosen to test his theories of socialization.

THE PHILOSOPHICAL ROOTS
OF OUTCOME-BASED EDUCATION

Outcome-based education is a philosophical umbrella under which there are several main content and methodological imperatives. There are several variations currently being implemented around the U.S. There are numerous applications and degrees of OBE, but at its roots, OBE claims to represent a new strategy which focuses on the outcome of a student's education. Because the application of OBE isn't uniform, it is important to understand both the philosophy and the people behind its development and implementation.

In the mid-fifties, professor Benjamin Bloom's book *A Taxonomy of Educational Objectives*, was published. In it, Bloom attempted to classify thinking from the lowest thinking to the highest or "critical" thinking. Bloom's taxonomy (way of classifying something) is the basis of OBE programs across the country today. According to Bloom, the desired result of teaching critical thinking is "...formulating subjective judgement as the end product resulting in personal values/opinions with no real right or wrong answer." So the highest achievement of critical thinking, according to Bloom, is moral relativism—no absolute truth. Bloom further explains that the purpose of good teaching is to change a student's "thoughts, feelings and actions.... The curriculum may be thought of as *a plan for changing student behavior*" (emphasis added).[2]

Ann Herzer, trained in mastery learning, says, "Outcome-Based Education is essentially a more advanced version of Professor Benjamin Bloom's Mastery Learning, which is pure Skinnerian, behaviorist, stimulus-response conditioning and indoctrination."[3]

Spady reinforces the direct link of outcome-based education to Bloom's relativistic, behavior-changing Mastery Learning:

> In January of 1980 we convened a meeting of 42 people to form the Network for Outcome-Based Schools. Most of the people who were there...had a strong background in Mastery Learning, since it was what OBE was called at the time. *But I pleaded with the group not to use the name "mastery learning" in the network's new name because the word "mastery" had already been destroyed* through poor implementation (emphasis added).[4]

In essence Spady is saying that if OBE is identified by its original name it will be rejected again. (Remember the Chicago disaster?) Notice how Spady takes no responsibility for the results in Chicago by declaring that "poor implementation" sabotaged the OBE effort there. Spady had to change the name of his theory, as well as repackage and re-market it, in order to make it seem like a new approach to an unaware, unsuspecting public.

Spady finds many soul-mates among the elite of the educational establishment. Shirley McCune is the senior director of the Mid-Continent Regional Educational Laboratory. This is a research and curriculum development nerve center (one of several funded by your tax dollars through the Department of Education). Here is McCune's explanation of her goal which she outlined at the national Governors' Conference on Education:

> *What we're into is the total restructuring of society.* What is happening in America today and what is

happening in Kansas and the Great Plains is not simply a chance situation in the usual winds of
change...it amounts to...a total transformation of
society...*you can't get away* from it. You can't go into
rural areas, you can't go into the churches, you can't
go into government or into business and hide
(emphasis added).[5]

McCune is calling for a complete overhaul of the structure of society. Rest assured she means your family too. Such
sweeping words from one as powerful as McCune are cause
for further inquiry. Why does McCune work to totally
restructure society? What would society look like if she had
her way? What are the goals behind the rhetoric?

Back in 1952 the National Training Laboratory (NTL)
became part of the National Education Association (NEA).
In 1968 the NTL became independent from the NEA but
never separated itself from its avowed purpose: "to change
teachers' inflexible patterns of thinking."[6] The philosophy of
the NTL is further outlined in their publications as the following quotations demonstrate:

Issues in Human Relations Training is published by
the NTL. In this book, the editors write that human
relations or sensitivity training "fits into a context of
institutional influence procedures which includes
coercive persuasion in the form of thought reform or
brainwashing...." The book also includes information about "change-agent skills" and "unfreezing,
changing and refreezing attitudes." And in David
Jenkins' essay in the book, he explains that the labo-
ratories conducted by the NTL have recently moved

from an emphasis on skill training to "sensitivity training," and he declares that "the trainer has no alternative but to manipulate; his job is to plan and produce behavior in order to create changes in other people." The manual also states regarding children that although "we appear to behave appropriately... this appearance is deceptive...[We are] 'pseudo-healthy' persons who can benefit from sensitivity training."[7]

In essence, your children may seem mentally healthy to most observers, but in actuality they will need the mental health care that only the NTL and their type can provide in order to conform to the centrally planned system these change-agents are working for.

In 1977 the NTL published a statement that clearly reveals the deceit they use to camouflage their agenda. "Volume 7, number 2 of *Social Change* [a newsletter from the NTL Institute for Applied Behavioral Science] contains an article by Massell Smith, who advises, 'Couch the language of change in the language of the status quo...Use the stated objectives of the status quo. They are almost broad enough to encompass innovation.'"

Another kindred spirit is John Goodlad who was the dean of the graduate school of education at the University of California at Los Angeles. Presently he is a professor at the University of Washington and president of the Institute for Educational Renewal. He wrote these words in the preface to James Becker's book *Schooling for a Global Age*:

Parents and the general public must be reached....
Otherwise, children and youth enrolled in globally

oriented programs may find themselves in conflict with values assumed in the home. And then the educational institution...comes under scrutiny....[8]

In a report Goodlad published, the following statement is made:

...Most youth still hold the same values as their parents and if we don't resocialize, our system will decay.[9]

Imagine that: Your children having the same values as you! How awful could it possibly be? Is this what we should be afraid of? Or should we stand against the philosophy of McCune, the National Training Laboratory, John Goodlad, and similarly minded individuals? Such people make tyranny possible. Minds charmed by a sense of destiny but possessing no sense of history are dangerous.

It doesn't matter how pure the intentions of those previously quoted may be. Good intentions are irrelevant. The good tutor, History, has given many graphic lessons about the revolution. One of the most poignant may be that it is never those who start the revolution (total restructuring) who see their ideals fulfilled over the long term. In the context of revolution, good intentions—fettered only by relativism—have a way of devolving into the lowest common denominator. Perhaps this is conceding too much. How could intentions be called good if they emanate from those whose grand designs insure their own supremacy?

A PLANNED SOCIETY

How far away are we from the road that leads to "conforming our children to the planned society," as the NTL describes the future they hope for? After reading the following statements carefully consider who uttered them:

A rough equality in general wealth and income is a necessary condition for equality of political power...

Most of the crimes that we know today would simply disappear under a socialist society.

No isolated subjects [taught] but [an] integrated viewpoint...greatest energies on actualizing talents and creativity....Students learn how to work and act together...no pressure to learn isolated facts...

The main emphasis will be on learning how to play, how to create, how to be an individual, and how to live and work collectively.

After the socialist revolution, education will have a much broader role. Every community will begin to develop facilities for extensive educational opportunities in all areas of human intellectual life...[10]

These statements were made in 1973 by Michael Lerner, a trusted associate of President Clinton and his wife. In the early 1970s Lerner led the Seattle Liberation Front, an ultra-Left organization described by the Washington State attorney general as "...totally indistinguishable from fascism and Nazism."[11] This statement was followed by an indictment of Lerner. Lerner is still openly opposed to free-market capitalism.

As recently as 1988 then-governor Bill Clinton wrote Lerner a letter saying, "You have helped me clarify my own thinking."[12] President and Mrs. Clinton have done nothing to distance themselves from Lerner. In fact they remain close associates to this day. If Lerner is one of the sources of inspiration for President Clinton's thinking and a trusted associate of both the President and his wife, is it extreme to be concerned with the growing federal involvement in education?

It seems that another group has also helped President Clinton to clarify his thinking. In his book *Chronology of Education,* Dr. Dennis Cuddy records the relationship between Bill Clinton and the NEA:

> July 2-5 [1993]: At the NEA's annual convention in San Francisco, delegates approved resolutions supporting "multicultural/global education," abortion-rights, and "comprehensive school-based clinics." Resolutions are also passed advocating teachers "be legally protected from censorship and lawsuits" related to sex education, including education regarding sexual orientation. Resolution B-1 states that "The NEA supports early childhood education programs in the public schools for children from birth through age eight." And concerning home schooling, Resolution B-58 indicates that "instruction should be by persons who are licensed by the appropriate state education licensure agency, and a curriculum approved by the state department of education should be used."

> President Clinton addresses the delegates and thanks the NEA for "the gift of our assistant secretary," referring to long-time NEA activist and staffer Sharon Robinson, who has become U.S. Assistant Secretary of Education for the Office of Educational Research and Improvement (OERI), and who sits

next to Hillary Clinton on the front row of the NEA convention. President Clinton goes on to say that he believes his goals for America closely parallel those of the NEA, further stating: *"And I believe that the president of this organization would say we have had the partnership I promised in the campaign of 1992, and we will continue to have it... You and I are joined in a common cause, and I believe we will succeed"*[3] (emphasis added).

In 1988 the National Center on Education and the Economy, a non-profit organization, was formed. Its purpose is to carry on the policy development work begun by the Carnegie Forum on Education and the Economy. Just before becoming First Lady, Mrs. Clinton, along with David Rockefeller and others, served as a director of the Center. In 1992 this organization circulated a confidential report entitled "The National Alliance for Restructuring Education: Schools—and Systems—for the 21st Century, A Proposal to the New American Schools Development Corporation by the National Center on Education and the Economy, Attn.: Marc Tucker, President." At the top of page thirty-three are the words, "How We Plan To Do It." The text on that page begins:

> *Our objective is to make schools of the kind we have described the norm,* not the exception, first in the cities and states that are Alliance members, and later elsewhere. *Getting there will require* more than new policies and different practices. It will require *a change in the prevailing culture—the attitudes, values, norms and accepted ways of doing things—that defines the environment* that determines whether individual

schools succeed or fail in the transformation process.
*We will know that we have succeeded when there are
enough transformed schools* in any one area, and
enough districts designed and managed to support
such schools, *that their approach to education sets the
norms, frames the attitudes and defines the accepted
ways of doing things in that part of the world. Then
there will be no turning back.*

*The question is how to bring about this kind of cultural
transformation on the scale we have in mind....*This
whole *design is calculated* to provide the *settings, relationships and people* resources needed for all phases of
learning we described, and *to organize them in such a
way that the growth of the new culture is geometric*
(emphasis added).

National associations, organizations, and the government—education's power brokers—are unified at a very basic
level. These outrageous statements are not being made by
the fringe element but by people in positions of power: the
people effecting change in your child's classroom...complete
societal change. Outcome-based education is seen as the
bridge to their desired future. The preceding quotes are a few
of many that demonstrate the mentality of those at the top of
education reform. These people believe it is their province to
orchestrate societal structure. As they have declared, they are
doing it through education. Every person mentioned above is
a proponent of Bill Spady's OBE restructuring effort.

It is time to consider how the philosophy of the ideo-
logues manifests itself in the implementation of OBE.

FOUR STAGES OF OBE

There are four stages of implementing outcome-based education. Don't get bogged down in some of the terms that seem unfamiliar. As you continue reading you will begin to see a pattern of repetition that you may be experiencing in your own district. The transition from one stage of OBE to the next is accomplished through patient gradualism. Spady defines the stages as follows:

STAGE 1: TRADITIONAL OBE
Focus: Subject area knowledge
(content: math, science, reading, etc.)

- discipline-driven outcomes
- mastery learning and outcome-based instruction
- A,B,I grading (eighty percent = mastery; incomplete (I) doesn't count on grade point average)
- teacher as audience (facilitator)

STAGE 2: LOW TRANSITIONAL OBE
Focus: Subject area with some processes
(still content-oriented, subject distinctions)

- future-driven competence outcomes (holistic perspective)
- traditional disciplines
- performance assessments (demonstration, open-ended tests, no multiple choice)
- teacher—created rubrics (scoring)
- self-assessment
- assessment of final product/some processes (group collaboration)
- A,B,I grading (eighty percent = mastery; incomplete doesn't count on grade point average)
- class as audience

Stage 3: High Transitional OBE

Focus: Processes and competencies authentically using subject matter (hands-on, real-life experience)

- future-driven competence outcomes from spheres (psychological, sociological, political)
- authentic, exit outcome-based performance assessments (portfolios, projects, etc.)
- traditional disciplines
- interdisciplinary (thematic, integrated)
- student- and teacher-created rubrics (scoring)
- self- and peer-assessment
- assess/validate processes and competencies
- criterion-based validation grading
- external experts as audience (community education, apprenticeship)

Stage 4: Transformational OBE

Focus: Functioning in life-roles (knowledge, competence, and orientation; community as school—what we want the student to be like—values)

- future conditions-driven life-role performance outcomes (psycho-socio-political focus)
- life sphere-driven curriculum structures (holistic, thematic, combining of subject matter)
- authentic role performances (apprenticeship, community service, working in community)
- student- and expert-created rubrics (business and industry will assess)
- validate competencies through authentic life-role performances (certificates of mastery, entry into work force, replace Carnegie unity)

- criterion validation, not grading (replacing grade with rubric and listed descriptions at each level of competency, no grade point average)
- external experts as audience (in community, working)

The following is a short vocabulary list that will help in understanding some of the new OBE terminology:

Outcome
: The direction or goal the student is to be moved toward.

Exit Outcome
: The conduct or behavior the student must demonstrate to the teacher's (facilitator's) satisfaction. The student's behavior reveals that he/she has assimilated the desired philosophy or information of a given outcome.

CIM
: Certificate of Initial Mastery. This certificate is received in lieu of the traditional graduation and diploma. It is awarded only after a successful demonstration of all outcomes. It is awarded at about the tenth grade level.

Strand
: The direction a student must choose after achieving the CIM. Students are typically fifteen or sixteen years old at this stage. Choosing the strand will establish the student's career path.

CAM
: Certificate of Advanced Mastery. This certificate is received after successful completion of year two of the strand program.

Bench Mark   The various grade levels where students are
                   assessed to determine how well they are pro-
                   gressing toward the Exit Outcomes.

Remediate   The process of continually returning the stu-
                   dent to the same material until he/she
                   demonstrates assimilation of the desired out-
                   come.

Non-Graded
Primary   The elimination of grade levels from kinder-
                   garten through third grade. All students
                   from this age group will be in the same class-
                   room. The primary method of learning is
                   developmentally appropriate practices
                   (DAP). This method does away with the tra-
                   ditional classroom setup and uses learning
                   stations where children "construct knowl-
                   edge" and engage in "self-directed learning."

Portfolio   There are two kinds of portfolios: Working
                   Portfolios and Electronic Portfolios. The
                   working portfolio is a collection of samples
                   of student work that the student, assisted by
                   the teacher, selects as the best examples of
                   his or her work throughout the year. The
                   electronic portfolio is computer-filed infor-
                   mation gathered on every student. This
                   information is student specific.

                   Portfolios contain not only academic
                   achievement, but also attitudes, beliefs, and
                   all medical records. The portfolio is designed

to follow the student into the job market. Potentially an employer would have electronic access to the cumulative information gathered over the years on a student now applying for a job.

Several tests that are designed for gathering portfolio information have been piloted in Oregon. One of these tests is "Wellness and Me: Portfolio project for lifetime health." Out of the one hundred questions on the test, there isn't one academic question. The last section of the test is called, "Looking at Values." Subsequent chapters will treat this topic in further detail. Suffice it to say that such tests are being used...and not only in Oregon.

ALL CHILDREN CAN LEARN

A primary supposition of outcome-based education is that, given enough time, all children can learn. Taken by itself this statement could be true. Yes, all children can learn...something. But in OBE this statement means all children can learn everything they are expected to learn. Such a standard sounds positive until it is analyzed. This assertion can't possibly be true unless a core of academic requirements is *not* part of the evaluation criteria. There are some students who simply do not have an aptitude for trigonometry, history, or perhaps, foreign language. To claim that all students can master high school physics is absurd. To suggest that all students could learn economics or learn to be excellent writers is beyond credibility. The elite OBE proponents are well aware of this, yet they press ahead with their declaration that "all children can learn." Why?

A review of the outcomes (chapter three) coupled with the philosophy of those behind OBE reveals why this claim can be made with logical impunity. Proponents of OBE make the seemingly irresponsible claim that all children can learn (everything) because at the core of transformational OBE one doesn't find a core of academics. This seems too absurd to be true, but consider the statements of two OBE proponents. Harvard Professor Anthony Oettinger has said:

> The present "traditional" concept of literacy has to do with the ability to read and write. But...do we really want to teach people to do a lot of sums or write...when they have a five-dollar hand-held calculator or a word processor? ...Do we really have to have everybody literate—writing and reading in the traditional sense...?[14]

Did you ever think you'd see the day when a professor from Harvard would suggest that writing and math aren't important? Couple this with the following quote where we see the interests of business specifically represented. Thomas B. Sticht, president and senior scientist, Applied Behavioral and Cognitive Sciences, Inc., San Diego, California, a member of the U.S. Secretary of Labor's Commission on Achieving Necessary Skills (SCANS) says:

> Many companies have moved operations to places with cheap, relatively poorly educated labor. What may be crucial, they say, is the dependability of a labor force and how well it can be managed and trained— not its general educational level, although a small cadre of highly educated creative people is essential to innovation and growth.

Ending discrimination and changing values are probably more important than reading and moving low-income families into the middle class (emphasis added).[15]

What Sticht is really saying is that we need more low-wage laborers in America. The only way to keep a pool of them available is to be sure that most students don't get educated. As long as the masses are poor and uneducated, the small cadre of highly educated, creative people can control them and have the kind of life they want. Sticht is calling for preparing a workforce with limited learning for life-long labor. Recognize this position for what it is. Either Sticht is a willing dupe who actually believes in the goodness of the "small cadre" or he is part of the small cadre and vying for power. You decide.

The current administration in the White House is in lockstep with Sticht and those of like mind. During the Bush administration, Hillary Clinton was on the board of directors for the National Center on Education and the Economy. This group was established by the Carnegie organization, the engine driving social change through education in this country. In June 1990, this group published a report called "America's Choice: High skills or low wages." This report calls for reformers to connect Labor with education. On page two, referring to America's business community, the report says:

...the system is managed by a small group of educated planners and supervisors who do the thinking for the organization. They plan strategy, implement changes, motivate the workers and solve problems. Extensive administrative procedures allow managers to keep control of a large number of workers.

Most employees under this model need not be educated.
It is far more important that they be reliable, steady and
willing to follow directions (emphasis added).

However this report was motivated, whatever they were trying to conclude, it seems clear that those responsible for it want those in power to see America's need for less-educated people. The report went on to say "the primary concern of more than 80 percent of employers was finding workers with a good work ethic and appropriate social behavior: reliable, a good attitude, a pleasant appearance, a good personality." Further, their statement reads, "More than 70 percent of the jobs in America will not require a college education by the year 2000." These statements are especially curious in light of the name of the report that contains them ("America's Choice: High skills or low wages"). But what is needed? Workers who do what they are told, with a good attitude. How are these happy, uneducated workers produced? Start now teaching students, from the earliest grades, the attitudes and social behaviors that will please business and avoid a broad-based, high quality, academic education.

CAN CHILDREN LEARN...EVERYTHING?

Let's go back to the question of whether all children can learn everything. From the above quotes, a distinct picture begins to emerge. The reason all children can learn under the transformational OBE system is because ultimately there is no core of academics for which they will be responsible (don't forget the four stages of implementation). The focus is on social behaviors that will enable them to function (at a minimal, dependant level) in the labor market. If you are still inclined to doubt the lack of content in transformational OBE, consider the following quote, again from Bill Spady, father of OBE, director of the International Center on Outcome-Based Restructuring and The High Success Network:

> I talk about two kinds of profound changes that need to happen if the system is going to be seriously outcome-based. One is, you have to stop being time-based. *The second is to stop being curriculum-based* (emphasis added).[16]

As you continue to learn more about OBE, it is important to know what the people at the top of education reform believe and the ideals for which they are working. In these first pages the attempt has been made to give you a basic introduction into the meaning and definitions used in OBE as well as the philosophy of several people at the top of education reform in this country.

There are as many motivations and intentions as there are people who are involved in education. Some have altruistic motives. Without understanding what is behind OBE, they embrace it, hoping to stop the hemorrhage of academic quality from American schools. As has been said, good intentions are, well, good. But when it comes to action, they are inconsequential. What matters is philosophy and what is done to inculcate that philosophy. An entire book could be filled with quotes similar to the ones above from other elite education theorists and change-agents currently working for the implementation of transformational outcome-based education.

What is important at this point is to understand the

motivations of those at the top of education reform in America. How did this most recent twist in education "reform" get started? Chapter two provides a recent history of the winds of change sweeping American education.

1. From Bill Spady's "High Success Network" seminar.

2. Benjamin Bloom, *All Our Children Learning* (New York: McGraw Hill, 1981) 180.

3. Ann Herzer quoted in *The New American,* 23 August 1993, 3.

4. William Spady interviewed in *Education Leadership,* December 1992-93.

5. Video tape of speech, Shirley McCune, Governors' Conference on Education, Kansas City, Mo., 1989.

6. Bill Jasper, *The New American,* August 1993, 4.

7. Dennis Laurence Cuddy, *Chronology of Education* (Highland City, Fl.: Pro Family Forum, 1994) 35.

8. John Goodlad, preface to *Schooling for a Global Age,* by James Becker (New York: McGraw Hill, 1979).

9. John Goodlad, *Schooling for the Future.* A report to the President's Commission of School Finance. *Educational Innovation,* issue 9, October 1971.

10. Michael Lerner, *The New Socialist Revolution: An introduction to theory and strategy* (Delacourt Press, 1973) 310-13.

11. Ambrose Evans-Pritchard, "White House gets cult fever: Bill and Hillary's guru in a yarmulke preaches Moses mixed with Marx," *The Sunday Telegraph,* June 1993.

12. Ibid.

13. Cuddy, *Chronology of Education,* 107.

14. Ibid., 4.

15. *House Journal,* 101st Cong., 1st sess., 23 October 1989.

16. Ron Brandt, "A Conversation with Bill Spady," *Educational Leadership,* December 1992/January 1993.

CHAPTER TWO

OBE

From the Federal Government to the Local District

I t has been over ten years since—after cries from parents across the nation protesting the quality of education, a continual decline of test scores, and increasing illiteracy— the National Commission of Excellence in Education was created. This commission, formed on August 26, 1981, was directed to report on the quality of education in America. By April 1983 the commission published a report called, *A Nation At Risk: The Imperative for Education Reform*:

> Our Nation is at risk. We report to the American people that, while we can take justifiable pride in what our schools and colleges have historically accomplished and contributed to the United States and the well being of its people, the educational foundations of our society are presently being eroded by a rising tide of mediocrity that threatens our very future as a Nation and as a people. What was

unimaginable a generation ago has begun to occur—others are matching and surpassing our educational attainments. *If an unfriendly foreign power had attempted to impose on America the mediocre educational performance that exists today, we might well have viewed it as an act of war.* As it stands, we have allowed this to happen to ourselves. We have even squandered the gains in student achievement made in the wake of the Sputnik challenge. Moreover, we have dismantled essential support systems which helped make those gains possible. *We have, in effect, been committing an act of unthinking, unilateral educational disarmament* (emphasis added).

With this amazing report, parents thought the way was paved for honest education reform. Finally American schools would return to a core of academic rigor and excellence that once catapulted American students to the pinnacle of success worldwide. Hope soared. Americans believed that students were going back to basics. No more experimental methods of instruction. The teaching of subjects that have little or nothing to do with academics would be curtailed. Academic standards would be raised and real achievement would be reinstated. A new, brighter day was about to dawn on the dark horizon of American education.

This report was presented over a decade ago. Has our system of education changed? Indeed it has, but not in the way most parents and other taxpayers hoped it would. A major shift in philosophy and methodology has been implemented. The entire emphasis of education has been altered. It is imperative that we understand the momentous changes occurring in education because culture and society will not go unaffected.

AMERICA 2000 BECOMES GOALS 2000...BUT WHAT CAME FIRST?

On March 5, 1990, the World Conference on Education for All (WCEFA) was held. This conference was sponsored by the United Nations Education, Scientific, and Cultural Organization, UNICEF, the United Nations Development Program, the World Bank, and other UN agencies. From the conference there came two documents: the World Declaration of Education for All and the Framework for Action to Meet Basic Learning Needs. The second document outlines six education goals. Following this conference, President George Bush held an Education Summit involving governors from every state. At this summit, six American national education goals were established. Curiously, five of the six goals were nearly identical in content to the goals established at the World Conference on Education for all.[1]

In April 1991, America 2000 was introduced in the U.S. Congress as education legislation. This bill created controversy and turmoil everywhere in America. President Bush, declaring himself the "Education President," planned to expand the role of the federal government in education. As vice president under Ronald Reagan, Bush was aware of Reagan's desire to eliminate the Department of Education. But that didn't happen primarily because of the influence of Terrel H. Bell who served as Reagan's Secretary of Education. Mr. Bell was part of the national educational establishment and had no intention of being a part of the dismantling of the department. Four years of conflict between the conservative administration and Mr. Bell ensued. In the end, the department remained—a relic of the deal struck between the National Education Association (NEA) and Jimmy Carter for the NEA's support in his bid for the presidency.

President Bush called together the nation's governors with the specific purpose of discussing education in America. Key players involved in this Education Summit were Governor Bill Clinton of Arkansas, Governor Madeline Kunin of Vermont, Governor Richard Riley of South Carolina, and Governor Lamar Alexander of Tennessee. The six National Educational Goals (NEG) and those from the World Conference on Education For All (WCEFA) are:

NEG 1:   By the year 2000, all children will start school ready to learn.

WCEFA 1:   Expansion of early childhood care and developmental activities, including family and community interventions, especially for poor, disadvantaged, and disabled children.

NEG 2:   By the year 2000, high school graduation rate will increase to at least ninety percent.

WCEFA 2:   Universal access to, and completion of, primary education (or whatever higher level of education each country considers as 'basic') by the year 2000.

NEG 3:   By the year 2000, American students will leave grades four, eight, and twelve having demonstrated competency in challenging subject matter including English, mathematics, science, history, and geography; and every school in America will ensure that all students learn to use their minds well, so they may be prepared for responsible citizenship, further learning and productive employment in our modern society.

WCEFA 3: Improvement in learning achievement at all grade levels. (The Framework for Action of WCEFA reads: "Such that an agreed percentage of an appropriate age cohort attains or surpasses a defined level of necessary learning achievement.")

NEG 4: By the year 2000, the U.S. will be first in the world in science and mathematics achievement.

WCEFA: No comparable goal.

NEG 5: By the year 2000, every adult will be literate and will possess the knowledge and skills necessary to compete in a global economy and exercise the rights and responsibility of citizenship.

WCEFA 4: Reduction of the adult illiteracy rate to at least one-half its 1990 level by the year 2000, with sufficient emphasis on female literacy to significantly reduce the current disparity between male and female illiteracy rates.

NEG 6: By the year 2000, every school in America will be free of drugs and violence and will offer a disciplined environment conducive to learning.

WCEFA 5:   Expansion of provision of basic education
            and training in other essential skills required
            by youth and adults with programme effec-
            tiveness assessed in terms of behavioral
            changes and impacts on health, employment,
            and productivity.

These goals may all seem good at first glance. Indeed, some of what is called for is laudable. Second looks, however, can be very revealing. To illustrate this point look again at the first goal: By the year 2000 all children will start school ready to learn. Starting school ready to learn appears to be a good idea until parents consider the implications of the second of three published objectives for this first goal, Objective 1:2: "Every parent in America will be a child's first teacher and devote time each day to helping his or her preschool child learn; parents will have access to the training and support they need."[2]

Who will evaluate whether parents are doing an adequate job of teaching their preschooler? What will the consequences be if they are found to be lacking? More important than these questions is the fundamental question, Who gave the responsibility for the well-being of children to the state—national or international? Children's well-being is not the province of the state. Starting school ready to learn is a good idea, but if it means that the state becomes the judge over individual cases, it invites abuse—not to mention the invasion of privacy and the destruction of personal freedom.

It is reasonable to wonder why the goals from the Governors' Conference are so similar to those that came out of the earlier World Conference. Was this merely an odd but unimportant coincidence?

When Mr. Clinton became president, those active in the Governor's Conference found new platforms of power from which to operate. The new Secretary of Education? Former Governor Richard Riley. The Deputy Secretary of Education? Former Governor Madeline Kunin. This group, in concert with the Clintons, created Goals 2000 which included the six educational goals from America 2000. This, however, was only the starting point.

A National Education Goals Panel, which serves to review education standards of individual states, was soon created. This panel has been aptly described as the new National School Board even though there is no constitutional sanction for this kind of invasion into the rights of individual states. Having no sanction is circumvented by a simple tactic—it's all based on voluntary participation by the states. An individual state's acceptance of the standards of the National Education Goals Panel is voluntary. However, as the power of the purse still rules, compliance is voluntary in name only. If the states want federal money for education (and no state could manage long without it), then the states must comply with the council's standards and authority.

SCANS: WHAT LABOR WANTS FROM EDUCATION

In May 1990, the U.S. Department of Labor created the Secretary's Commission on Achieving Necessary Skills (SCANS). Appointed as the executive director of SCANS, Arnold Packer was already known for his 1987 report "Workforce 2000: Workers for the 21st century." In June 1991, one month before Oregon's education reform became law, SCANS published its first report entitled, "What Work Requires of Schools: A SCANS report for America 2000."

This raised questions: Why was the Department of Labor dictating to education? Was this a portent of things to come?

On page six of this booklet (available from your local government print shop) are the workplace competencies:

Resources   They know how to allocate time, money, materials, space, and staff.

Interpersonal
Skills   They can work on teams, teach others, serve customers, lead, negotiate, and work well with people from culturally diverse backgrounds.

Information   They can acquire and evaluate data, organize and maintain files, interpret and communicate, and use computers to process information.

Systems   They understand social, organizational, and technological systems; they can monitor and correct performances; and they can design or improve systems.

Technology   They can select equipment and tools, apply technology to specific tasks, and maintain and trouble-shoot equipment.

On the same page, foundational skills are identified:

Basic Skills   Reading, writing, arithmetic and mathematics, speaking, and listening.

Thinking
Skills   The ability to learn, reason, think creatively, make decisions, and solve problems.

Personal
Qualities   Individual responsibility, self-esteem and self-
                   management, sociability, and integrity.

Few workers meet all these qualifications. As you continue reading it is demonstrated through comparison that the above definitions are part of the pool of definitions from which OBE proponents draw. This is OBE rhetoric from the outset. It sounds good, but the reality is that outcome-based education, which lacks rigorous academic content, is not capable of producing this kind of worker...even if Labor did have the right to make demands of secondary education. None of these competencies or skills, or their extended definitions, emphasize the individual's initiative or creativity. The focus is only on the group or the individual's contribution to the group.

The next report published by SCANS was "Learning a Living" (April 1992), followed by "Teaching the SCANS Competencies" (1993). The last report expanded the definitions of the five competencies and also explained the plan for implementing its requirements into school curriculum. President Bush's America 2000 (which, incidentally, did focus on academic improvement) became President Clinton's Goals 2000, which led to school-to-work legislation.

The *School-to-Work bill* actually requires a national school-to-work opportunities system that is based on national skill standards. As with the National Education Goals Panel, included in the *School-to-Work bill* is the requirement of state mandates, which find protection in the shadow of the word *voluntary*. If you don't volunteer to comply, you don't receive any federal funds. After the money is accepted the law reads definitively with words like "shall," "every," "all," and "must." The SCANS commission provides their recommendations to the states—in many cases, coupled with financial incentives to comply, voluntarily.

Another consideration is that the government's effort to control is not limited to students, schools, teachers, and businesses. This system calls for "assessing and certifying those already in the work force."[3] H.B. 2884 (school-to-work legislation) was summarized in *Education Week* magazine:

> Learning must include matching students with employers, liaisons among students, employers, teachers, (the school will assist the child getting a first job) placing program graduates into jobs, linking participants with other community service. Collecting information on students progress after graduation...up-grading skills of existing workers."[4]

Employees currently in the workplace will also be subject to evaluation and certification requirements. Once this system is in place, will there be any way to avoid the control it necessarily brings with it? Allow the government to mandate the SCANS competencies into the educational process, and effectively the Department of Labor has been allowed to dictate the goals, quality, and content of education for our children. Though this approach enjoys positive press, it is difficult to avoid suspicion that behind the smiles of its promoters is the continuing effort of government to usurp local control of education.

Whatever the impetus behind these federal government efforts, there seems to be a collective pull in one direction—OBE for all students K-12. Is it possible that those influencing education in America seized the opportunity of the national outcry for academic excellence to make another colossal change in the opposite direction? Parents and other taxpayers have been united: "Give students a solid academic education." Are OBE proponents using parents' hope for academic excellence to create a system of training, as opposed to educating?

To help answer this question, consider the published outcomes from several states around the country...the subject of chapter three.

1. Ed and Mary Tarkowski, *Education Reform: It Ain't Just a Local Thing,* May 1993, 6-7.

2. U.S. Department of Education, *America 2000,* 37.

3. SCANS report: *Learning a Living,* 15.

4. *Education Week,* 26 January 1994, 18.

Outcomes...

The Real Content of Transformational OBE

A cross our country the outcomes being implemented in each state are suspiciously parallel; their content is effectively identical. In most cases, as revealed by the outcomes list in this chapter, the outcomes deal with attitudes, values, and behaviors. When solid subjects like math and science are included, the emphasis is not on content but rather on process. Outcomes are the goals and direction which the child is moved toward. These outcomes drive the system and are the cornerstone of the laws being introduced around the country.

SO, EXACTLY WHAT IS AN OUTCOME?

An outcome is a broad category of behavior and skills that a student must demonstrate. Whereas students used to be required to demonstrate their knowledge in a particular subject, say math, now they must exhibit "mastery of an outcome." Consider two examples of outcomes from Oregon:

Outcome	Explanation
Understand diversity	understand human diversity and communicate in a second language, applying appropriate cultural norms
Collaborate	participate as a member of a team, including providing leadership for achieving goals and working well with others from diverse backgrounds

Bill Spady says that outcomes are designed around the future. Educators pushing OBE look at the future and design backwards based on the needs of the future as they perceive them. Once they think they have an understanding of the demands for the future, they come up with a set of performance objectives (outcomes). After a quick look at the outcomes it is clear that they revolve around what kids will need to be like, not what they need to know. Currently there are outcomes from more than forty states where OBE is being or has been implemented. While most state departments of education are claiming that their outcomes are unique, the menu of outcomes available nationwide gives away the truth.

Since it is the outcomes that become the basis for receiving one's diploma (certificate of mastery), their importance is paramount. They replace academic subjects. Consider the focus of your child's school day consisting of subjects such as identifying the community's problems, civil rights defended worldwide, solving interpersonal problems and conflicts, using the environment responsibly, being worldwide citizens, understanding and accepting diversity.

Children will be assessed based on their changing attitudes toward these subjects. All occurs under the auspices of the child's self-esteem which is considered paramount to all other considerations. The definitions of these subjective subjects must be based on someone's political viewpoint. The question is, Whose? Do you suppose it will be the parent's viewpoint? Or would it perhaps be the viewpoint of the majority of the community? Whose values will be used to determine if the child has assimilated the philosophy of the outcome or is exhibiting the correct behavior?

HOW CAN THE OUTCOMES BE THE SAME EVERYWHERE? I WAS TOLD THEY WERE LOCALLY DETERMINED.

During the phase of implementation designed to make people comfortable with the outcomes, citizens from Pennsylvania to Oregon were told the outcomes were locally determined. Even after a quick look at the published information it is clear that the outcomes represent a cohesive effort to move to a nationalized system of education. If this is not the case, how did the outcomes end up being the same from state to state? It appears that the guiding hand of government was heavily involved.

The outcomes from more than forty states are nearly identical in content. To acquire a first-hand understanding of this, take some time to compare the following outcomes from various states. The listing order and wording varies, but that is where their dissimilarities end. The point of listing the many state outcomes is not to analyze whether individual outcomes are good or bad, but to demonstrate that they are the result of a collective effort across the nation. When a national school board is coupled with a list of national education outcomes, it amounts to a national system of education. A short key is provided to aid comparison of the outcomes. The letter identifies the state and the number identifies which outcome under that state is similar to others on the same line.

COMPARE   I 1, O 6, G 2, T 4
          I 2, T 7, G 5
          I 3, O 8, T 6, G 4
          I 4, O 11, T 1&10
          I 5, O 3, T 5, G 6
          I 6, O 2, T 8, G 4
          I 7, O 1, T 3, G 1

INDIANA

1. Work cooperatively and independently.
2. Contribute positively to community and society.
3. Demonstrate respect for self and uniqueness of others.
4. Practice physical, social, and mental wellness.
5. Communicate effectively.
6. Accept responsibility for learning.
7. Utilize creativity, problem solving, and critical thinking.

OREGON

1. Think: Think critically, creatively, and reflectively in making decisions and solving problems.

2. Self-direct learning: Direct his or her own learning, including planning and carrying out complex projects.

3. Communicate: Communicate through reading, writing, speaking, and listening, and through an integrated use of visual forms such as symbols and graphic images.

4. Use technology: Use current technology, including computers, to process information and produce high-quality products.

5. Quantify: Recognize, process, and communicate quantitative relationships.

6. Collaborate: Participate as a member of a team, including providing leadership for achieving goals and working well with others from diverse backgrounds.

7. Deliberate on public issues: Deliberate on public issues which arise in our representative democracy and in the world by applying perspectives from the social sciences.

8. Understand diversity: Understand human diversity and communicate in a second language, applying appropriate cultural norms.

9. Interpret human experience: Interpret human experience through literature and the visual and performing arts.

10. Apply science
    and math: Apply science and math concepts and
                    processes, showing an understanding
                    of how they affect our world.

11. Understand
    positive health
    habits: Understand positive health habits
                    and behaviors that establish and
                    maintain healthy interpersonal rela-
                    tionships.

TEXAS

1. Exhibit self-esteem and adaptability in real world situations.

2. Access, process, and evaluate information from a
   variety of resources, including technology.

3. Use critical thinking and self-directed learning skills
   throughout life.

4. Demonstrate problem-solving, decision-making, and
   group-process skills.

5. Demonstrate effective communication skills.

6. Demonstrate respect and concern for self and others
   in culturally diverse work, community, and family
   settings.

7. Demonstrate personal, social, civic, economic, and
   environmental responsibility.

8. Exhibit positive work habits, attitudes, and ethics.

9. Be motivated producers who create and appreciate
   quality, intellectual, artistic, and practical products.

10. Formulate positive core values in order to set goals and create a vision for the future.

GEORGIA

1. Complex thinker— who produces solutions to real life problems based on assembly and integration of data from a variety of sources.

2. Collaborative contributor— who cooperates effectively in a variety of settings and with a diversity of people.

3. Innovative producer— who creates quality ideas, solutions, or products using effective skills for gathering and organizing information.

4. Self-directed achiever— who develops self-respect by accomplishing personal goals based on high standards.

5. Involved citizen— who accepts responsibility for contributing time and talent toward community and global affairs to enhance the quality of life for all.

6. Effective communicator—who informs, expresses self, and persuades by sending and receiving verbal and non-verbal languages.

These outcomes are not just similar, they are the same. The reason? OBE is becoming a national curriculum. What is wrong with a national system of education controlled by the federal government? Nothing, so long as the government restrains itself from attempts to invade and control the personal lives of its citizens. Such a notion is sheer fantasy. Government doesn't possess the capacity to restrain itself... something the founders of this nation recognized and which prompted them to write the founding documents the way they did. The federal government has no constitutional sanction to involve itself in education. The Tenth Amendment to the Constitution says, "The powers not delegated to the United States by the Constitution, nor prohibited by it to the States, are reserved to the States respectively, or to the people."[1] Education has never been assigned as a responsibility of the federal government.

James Madison gave the grave warning that, among other things, the government may attempt to "take into their hands the public education of children...Were the power of Congress to be established in the latitude contended for [i.e. government controlling the education of children] it would subvert the very foundations, and transmute the very nature of the limited government established by the people of America."[2] The founders knew that letting the federal government involve itself in education was fraught with danger to the freedom of citizens. This is why they did everything they could to design a system that would keep the federal government out of education. But the government has every intention to be deeply involved with education at every level. Consider the following letter from G. Leland Burningham, the state superintendent of public instruction for Utah. This letter was written on July 27, 1984 to T. H. Bell, President Reagan's Secretary of Education:

> I am forwarding this letter to accompany the proposal which you recommended Bill Spady and I prepare in connection with Outcome-Based Education.
>
> This proposal centers around the detailed process by which *we will work together to implement Outcome-Based Education* using research verified programs. *This will make it possible to put outcome-based education in place, not only in Utah but in all schools of the nation.* For those who desire, *we will stand ready for regional and national dissemination of the Outcome-Based Education program.*
>
> We are beginning to see positive, preliminary results from some of the isolated schools in Utah which have implemented Outcome-Based Education. These positive indicators are really exciting! (emphasis added)

As I have said, Spady is known as the father of OBE. This letter reveals that Bell recommended Spady and Burningham submit a proposal for federal funding (which they received) for a plan making it possible to put OBE in every school of the nation. Clearly these are the building blocks of a national system of education.

The aforementioned outcomes are the areas in which students will have to demonstrate mastery before they can receive their certificate of initial mastery. In a few of the outcomes academics are mentioned, but even then the emphasis is not on content but on process. It is difficult for someone who has had any amount of traditional education to look at these outcomes and understand how it is possible that these will become the focus of the learning day.

Even if Americans were to accept an education system that minimized the role of academic knowledge, is it wise to allow such subjective outcomes to be the basis on which students are to be assessed? In a word, no! Anita Hoge asks five vital questions that reveal the dangers of such a system:[3]

1. How do you measure that outcome?

For example: If an outcome states that "all children must have ethical judgment, honesty, or integrity," what exactly is going to be measured? How do you measure a bias in a child? Must children be diagnosed? Will they be graded by observation or take a pencil-and-paper test? How will performance or behavior be assessed?

2. How is that outcome scored, or what is the standard?

What behavior is "appropriate" and to what degree? For example, how much self-esteem is too much or not enough to graduate? Can government score the attitudes and values of its citizens?

3. Who decides what that standard will be?

The state has extended its mandated graduation requirement, or exit outcomes, down to the individual child. This bypasses all local autonomy. What about locally elected school directors—will they become obsolete? Are we talking about a state or government diploma?

4. How will my child be remediated?

What are you going to do to my children to change them from here to there in their attitudes and values in order to graduate? How do you remediate ethical judgment, decision making, interpersonal skills, environmental attitudes? What techniques will be used? What risks are involved? What justification does the state have to change my child's attitudes?

5. What if parent and state disagree on the standard or how it is measured in the classroom?

Who has the ultimate authority over the child...parents or the state? What about privacy? Can parents opt out of a graduation requirement mandated by the state?

In transformational outcome-based education these outcomes become the primary thrust, not a math class or a science class. Even many teachers have a hard time accepting this idea, which is why the National Training Laboratory is committed to "change teachers' inflexible patterns of thinking."[4] This statement from the NTL reveals their disdainful view of teachers' attitudes.

It is disingenuous to paint the entire spectrum of teachers with the broad, negative stroke of a brush when they are the ones the NTL relies upon to implement their social agenda. It is also unfair in the extreme. Many teachers in American public schools work under a tremendous load of large classrooms and no provision for student discipline which makes their task nearly impossible. Some of the teachers I know are the most creative, hard-working people I have ever met. There is nothing inflexible about the way they teach. I would encourage teachers as a whole to consider the attitude behind such statements as that made by the NTL. Upon closer consideration it may be apparent that the teacher is only a pawn in their game of social revolution.

Many people involved with schools that have begun to implement OBE will protest that this is not what they are doing. It may well not be what they are doing...now. Remember there are four stages to the implementation of OBE. Those schools have not yet reached the transformational stage of OBE, but that is where they are headed because that is where the federal government and other change-agents are taking education.

What has been demonstrated is that the outcomes in varying states across America are not only academically deficient, but they are also identical in real content. This is simply too coincidental not to have been engineered by the federal government and other national organizations. This level of uniformity creates a dangerous potential of inviting increasing government control over education...control that the federal government is positioning itself to usurp.

1. The Constitution of the United States of America.

2. Annals of Congress. February 2, 1791.

3. Anita Hoge, excerpted from "How Do You Measure that Outcome?" *Education Week*, November 10, 1993.

4. Purpose statement of the National Training Laboratory as quoted in *The New American*, August 1993, 5.

CHAPTER FOUR

The New OBE School

here are major changes being planned for the school site, but because there is a plethora of think-tanks, foundations, and government agencies that are involved in the change of education, it is impossible to look to one source and find a definitive list of what is intended. What can be done is to look for patterns that repeat themselves from group to group.

And like the African proverb says, "*It takes a whole village to raise a child.*" If you haven't seen or heard this statement recently, you will. It is one of many new mantras of the elite change agents in the education establishment working to create a society more to their liking. Understanding the real meaning of the proverb as opposed to the way it is being used requires a closer look.

The idea of village and community is a warm one indeed. As America grows more fractured, people have a greater longing to find community. The phrase has a quaint, home-spun quality and no doubt represents much truth in its original context. What is the original context of the proverb? The extended family. The African village is an extended family. Grandparents, parents, uncles, aunts, cousins, brothers, and sisters make up the African village. The Amish community in America provides an excellent parallel, one in which the proverb would likewise apply.

What is appropriate and good in one context can be inappropriate and even bad in another. The reason this proverb was chosen is because OBE promoters intend to make the school location a village—the full-service community where your child will be raised. The following words were taken from a document that was circulated among Oregon middle schools:

> Each school will provide a small community for its students. This community should be a safe place where close, trusting relationships with adults and peers create a climate for personal growth and intellectual development. Within this supportive environment, the curriculum will provide first hand opportunities for exploration and investigation, and will be based on the developmental needs of the students.[1]

This piece of public record is calling for the school "community" to replace the family. Increasingly, teachers are being told that they must provide for all of the needs of the students. There is an OBE solution for every student need. But is every area of student need the jurisdiction of the school? If the school focuses on all possible student needs when will there be time to focus on academics? Furthermore, should the school become a government agency dispensary?

A recent special advertising section of *Newsweek* magazine was entitled, "Education in America." The lead article was written by Pat Henry, National PTA President, 1991-93. After praising "Hillary Rodham Clinton's long history of involvement in children's issues," Henry correctly stated that one of the most vital elements of education in America is parental involvement. But then he went on to make the statement, "We can't leave it to parents. But we can't leave it to schools. You and I must get involved…"[2]

It is stated fairly mildly here but OBE moves parents to the sidelines. If "it" (reaching National Education Goals by the year 2000) can't be left to parents and teachers, who else needs to be invited to the party? The National PTA's "A National Agenda For Children" makes it very clear:

2. Commission a National Children's Summit and create a White House office for Children. Summit participants would propose comprehensive national youth and family policy.

4. Enact a comprehensive early-childhood education policy [federal level] that strengthens children's physical and mental health.

The main article of this publication was written by James P. Comer, director of the School Development Program at Yale Child Study Center, and associate dean of Yale School of Medicine. The illustration accompanying this article is a puzzle. When put together the picture the puzzle makes is of a young girl, off to school with a back pack slung over her shoulders. There are a few pieces to the puzzle not yet in place. Written on the three unplaced pieces is "Teachers," "Community" and "Parents." Remember, it takes a whole village, in fact, the entire government, to raise your child. In

his article, "The Community Classroom," Dr. Comer
declares:

> Parents, schools and community groups must sys-
> tematically create the society of caring adults in and
> around school that once existed in a natural
> way…these initiatives involve young people with car-
> ing adults who guide them in academic learning and
> social development and, in some cases, introduce
> them to college and mainstream work opportuni-
> ties—worlds unknown to their parents.[3]

Parents, you see, are rather out of it and are only a part
of the puzzle of raising a child anyway. As long as a caring
adult can be found to guide the child in social development,
parents fade to the background. It takes a whole village, after
all, to raise a child. There is, however, a fundamental problem with the comparison. The OBE village isn't composed of
extended family. It is made up of government services with
offices right on the school sight.

The philosophy of those pushing OBE identifies the
school as community. The school site becomes the focal
point of the students' and parents' lives. It is the center of
community activities. Because all students will become lifelong learners, it is necessary to establish the super learning-
community center. This is why there are plans on the books
of many states to bring all social services to the school site.

This policy is backwards for a very simple reason. When
it comes to government services, access always encourages
excess. Government handouts are as addictive as any drug.
Don't misunderstand. Those who need social services should
get them. But let us not forget that the ease of access always

encourages abuse. This is the very reason that the federal government is currently trying to find a way to curtail welfare benefits. The system is being severely abused.

Furthermore, most people in real need of social services are not high school students. Why are social planners behind OBE trying to get addictive social services established at the school sites? It looks like a further effort to make the student population a ward of the state. What happens when an angry teen has a blow-up with a parent? Instead of staying at home to work it out with mom and dad, under the new system, he or she can run to the social service office, find shelter, food, condoms, a "caring adult," and anything else needed to avoid going back home. OBE proponents claim to be concerned about kids from broken homes and to support the family, but when such policies are enacted they actually work to weaken and de-emphasize the family.

ALL GOVERNMENT SOCIAL SERVICES ON THE SCHOOL SITE

Imagine for a moment the far-reaching hand of the state touching the lives of all children who enter the doors of a government school. The day begins with being dropped off at school. Stepping through the doorway-to-the-future, students see before them the hallway of life-support where every need they could possibly have is met.

First, on the left, is the welfare office assuring all necessary meals. The food stamp office, where aid will be available for lunches or dinner purchased off the school site, is just across the hall. Close at hand is the medical services and public health center. The convenient location makes a quick stop to pick up free condoms easy. Young ladies are stopping briefly at the child-care center to drop off their babies. The sheriff's branch office has everyone backed up at the metal detectors. Only a little further to go now past the teen health clinic where abortions are encouraged and the drug detox center helps kids sober up. Finally students arrive at the education wing where carefully chosen, academically-impaired subject matter helps to shape their values and attitudes.

If you think this is an alarmist view, read carefully these next few words from Shirley McCune, senior director of the Mid-Continent Regional Educational Lab. This curriculum development institution is one hundred percent behind OBE. McCune has been referred to as the high priestess of OBE. Read and understand the OBE vision in her own words in a keynote speech at the 1989 Governors' Conference on Education:

> When you walk in the building, there's a row of offices. In one are drug counselors, one is for social security...schools are no longer in the schooling business, but rather in the human resource development...*we have an opportunity to develop the kind of society we want* (emphasis added).[4]

McCune wasn't being frivolous when, at the same conference, she said, "We...are into...the total restructuring of society."

The dreams of the education establishment elite are now finding their way into local districts. In Oregon, the state guidelines for implementing H.B. 3565, the *Outcome-Based Education bill* now passed into law, were developed under the auspices of the state department of education. The guidelines call for the integration of "school and social services for children and families."[5] What is to be provided?

Comprehensive social services. In the words of the guidelines report, these services are defined as "education and all other programs and services addressing one or more of a child's six basic needs as follows: stimulus, nutrition, health, safety, nurturance and shelter."[6]

Another encroachment on the family has just occurred. These areas are the domain of the family. It is the family that has the primary responsibility for the welfare of the child. But those pushing OBE are interested in "total restructuring." Are you willing to acquiesce to the government's efforts to gain more control over you and your family?

Some social planners believe it is best if they reach into the American family and control it from cradle to grave. These and their ilk are convinced that they know what you need for every phase of your life and are determined to give it to you. They believe that parents and extended families can't handle life around them, so the state should step in. With this gross assumption on the part of the interventionists, the state then allows the parent to become partners in parenting. Big of them, don't you think?

Beware of those who ensure their own supremacy by what they advocate. With the advent of the full spectrum of social services at school, parents will be trading the sovereignty of parenthood for government intervention in family life. It's a bad bargain. It will take one or two generations of government social services on the school site before the misused African proverb becomes rigid belief.

1. This quote is from an untitled, undated document that was circulated at G. Russell Middle School in Gresham, Oregon. Spring 1993, 8.

2. Pat Henry, "Finally: Children First," *Newsweek*, Special Advertising Section, 5.

3. James P. Comer, "The Community Classroom," *Newsweek*, Special Advertising Section.

4. Video tape of speech, Shirley McCune, Governors' Conference on Education, Kansas City, Mo., 1989.

5. "Integration of Social Services," *Task Force Report*, Oregon Department of Education, Salem, Oregon, January 1993.

6. Ibid., 2.

CHAPTER FIVE

The New Teacher in the New Classroom Using the New Method

f the designation *teacher* isn't on the way out, at least the definition is. The term "teacher" in the OBE system doesn't mean what you thought it meant. To help in understanding the new responsibilities of teachers the following list is provided, courtesy of the Oregon Department of Education:

1. Provides the environment to meet student needs.
2. Assures emotionally and physically safe and secure environment.
3. Observes and assesses student's learning and development.
4. Encourages student development of understanding and competence.
5. Mediates learning.
6. Introduces experiences, models; extends thinking.
7. Capitalizes on the experiences and individuality of students.

8. Values effort.
9. Communicates within child's environment to promote the coordinated effort of all concerned for the student's good.

The above list was presented in workshops by "distinguished Oregon educators" (i.e. OBE proponents). As one readily observes, actually teaching the kids is out. Teachers no longer impart knowledge. In fact under OBE it is critical that they do not. As the father of OBE, William Spady, has said, the outcome-based system must "stop being curriculum-based."[1] It requires little imagination to anticipate the result of teachers not teaching content but rather facilitating the exploration of children's curiosities.

DEVELOPMENTALLY APPROPRIATE PRACTICES

Outcome-based education has a comrade-in-arms that calls for a new way of educating young students. It is known as developmentally appropriate practices or DAP. While DAP is not technically connected to outcome-based education, proponents of OBE consider DAP imperative to the education of young children, which is why it accompanies the implementation of OBE everywhere in the U.S. What are developmentally appropriate practices? The National Association for the Education of Young Children has outlined DAP as follows:[2]

Practice: There is an integrated curriculum where learning in all traditional subject areas occurs primarily through projects, learning centers, and play activities.

Meaning: No more directive teaching. No more content teaching. Young students will learn on their own by doing fun activities. In this model learning simply occurs, students don't strive to acquire knowledge.

Practice: Children learn through active involvement with each other, with adults and older children serving as informal tutors.

Meaning: Children learn from each other, not the teacher. The new role for the teacher is a passive tutor or facilitator. Older students are used as passive tutors as well.

Practice: Individual children or small groups work and play cooperatively or alone in learning centers on projects that they usually select themselves.

Meaning: Children self-direct their "learning." They are not directed by a teacher to do anything they don't want to do. Generally it is inappropriate for the teacher to select work for the student to accomplish.

Practice: Learning materials and activities are concrete, real, and relevant to children's lives.

Meaning: The child decides what is relevant.

Practice: The math program enables children to use math through exploration, discovery, and solving relevant problems.

Meaning: No direct teaching and no rote learning of how to do sums or requiring the memorization of multiplication tables. Children will "explore" these subjects at learning centers.

Practice: Social studies themes are identified as the focus of work for extended periods of time and are learned through a variety of projects and playful activities involving independent research through reading, excursions, discussions, relevant use of language, etc.

Meaning: No directive teaching of content.

Practice: Discovery science is a major part of the curriculum.

Meaning: Children will discover through exploration. Again, there is no teaching of specific science content.

Practice: Art, music, movement, and drama are integrated activities in the learning process.

Meaning: Self-evident.

Practice: Teachers promote socialization behavior, perseverance, industry, and independence by providing many stimulating and motivating activities.

Meaning: Students begin to learn how to exhibit the behaviors required of them by outcomes.

Practice: Teachers promote the development of children's conscience and self-control through positive guidance techniques, including setting clear limits in a positive manner and involving children in establishing rules for their class and social living.

Meaning: Self-evident.

Practice: Teachers build on the child's internal motivation and interest.

Meaning: The non-directive efforts of the teacher/facilitator are based on what motivates the child and what the child is interested in.

Practice: Teachers view and accept parents as partners.

Meaning: The primary responsibility for the children lies with the school. Parents are only one part of a multi-faceted process. "Viewing" and "accepting" parents as partners establishes the teacher and school as the center of control. Parents must fit into the system and know their proper place.

Practice: Children are not retained without detailed rationale determined by an interdisciplinary team that supports the action.

Meaning: Make every effort to keep a student from failing a grade.

Practice: Pullout programs are discouraged and care is taken to integrate special needs children into all classroom activities.

Meaning: Students with severe learning and physical disabilities will not be given special attention for their educational needs. They will be mainstreamed, i.e. be present with all other children in the same class.

There is one more element to the complex web of this new method of instruction. It is called *mixed-age grouping* and is considered the logical extension of DAP.[3] In other words, wherever DAP is found, so is mixed-age grouping. And DAP is found wherever OBE is found. Mixed-age grouping calls for the combining of children from kindergarten through third grade into the same classroom. In effect mixed-age grouping calls for classrooms made up of boys and girls, ages five to eight.

Don't forget that all of the severely mentally and emotionally disabled children of those same ages will be in the classroom as well. This is double jeopardy. Disabled children need special, focused attention. They will never get it in this environment. While the disabled students lose out, so do the other children as attention invariably focuses on the child making the greatest stir, disrupting the class. With this system everyone loses. If it were true that the education of children is first and foremost, as the OBE proponents claim, why are they calling for such a disorganized, disruptive learning environment?

To most people such grouping of various aged children sounds like planned chaos. As ridiculous as it seems, it's as if a group of social planners was given the goal of developing a system that would insure young children wouldn't and couldn't become educated. If the goal is to keep the children from learning, these methods will attain it.

Developmentally appropriate practices and non-graded primary are confused, convoluted concepts. How does the teacher organize a day of learning? What is used as the standard by which to assess student progress? The above guidelines describe nothing more than a continuous play-time atmosphere. Is this the type of atmosphere you want your children in until they are seven or eight years old? Most parents would rather have their children learn how to read and write.

Self-directed learning may be a good idea for the postgraduate researcher, but for the primary student it raises some serious questions. What are Johnny and Sue interested in today? What do they feel like learning today?

Because of the learning center imperative as opposed to the traditional approach of the teacher teaching, the physical classroom changes. Instead of the organized environment where students' desks face a teacher who teaches a body of knowledge to the kids for which they will be accountable, there are now learning stations around the room. In many cases desks are non-existent. At these learning stations the student picks what he or she feels like learning that day. This learning environment is a natural response to the belief that "children construct knowledge."[4]

In DAPs there are play stations, rest stations, and subject stations (the variety of stations is limited only by the imagination of the teacher) through which the child is free to explore the world of learning. Children in this stage are five to eight years old. How are they supposed to legitimately explore the world of learning? As Gladys Hunt points out in her tremendously insightful and valuable book, *Honey for a Child's Heart,* "When children are small and don't know what is valuable…that is an agonizing responsibility to place on a child."[5]

It is abject nonsense to turn a child loose with children of various ages and expect that that child will "construct knowledge." But what is worse is to then call such an educational charade learning. Human nature would have a six year old at the play station most of the time.

KIDS SET THE ACADEMIC STANDARD?

Parents have too much experience to accept that young children are going to set for themselves academic goals and standards and then discipline themselves to attain those goals. This would be learning in a void. It doesn't happen. As long as you don't take human nature into account, this system would work well. Sensible people know that anything worthwhile takes work to attain. Good teachers make the work of learning to read and write enjoyable because they are gifted with enthusiasm, creativity, and the capacity to help students believe in themselves. There is no substitute for good education and good teaching.

Students left to themselves will learn what they feel like learning. Undoubtedly these kids' interests will span the spectrum of subjects. Different levels of intelligence and stages of learning will be the norm, not to mention the differences in maturity between five-year-old boys and eight-year-old girls. How would you like to be the teacher in the fourth grade who picks these kids up with absolutely no standardization? It is a catastrophe occurring in a nightmare—especially for a child's real educational prospects.

PUBLIC SCHOOLS DON'T TEACH KIDS
HOW TO SOUND OUT WORDS

Further confusion is added to education by the refusal to teach children how to sound out words. Reading skills have been on the decline for decades. This is a precarious trend because reading well is the infrastructure upon which all quality education rests. All other educational concerns will not matter if children don't have the foundation of reading with which to approach other subjects.

The debate is between phonics and whole language. For a few decades now, whole language has been the predominant method of teaching kids to read. As you may already know, whole language is teaching children to point along at the words of a text and memorize the most common ones. There is no attempt to sound out the word because the child doesn't know anything about the sounds associated with the letters or their relationship to words. The idea is to look at the word and say it. The child needs to memorize anywhere from 350 to 1500 of the most commonly used words. Children are allowed to substitute different words which have essentially the same meaning. For example, a child may substitute the word "father" with "dad" because it means the same thing. This example was given to me by a teacher who uses whole language.

Even if there are some successes with whole language, it cannot serve most children well into their futures. How will they be able to learn new words and vocabulary that they will inevitably encounter later in life when they haven't learned the different sounds letters can make? Certainly it encourages a static vocabulary.

Like DAP and non-graded primary, whole language isn't technically connected to OBE. However, as with these other practices, it accompanies OBE wherever it is implemented.

The 1989 National Assessment of Educational Progress report revealed that "two out of three 17-year-olds could not read well enough to do high school work in any subject."

The report went on to trace the history of American literacy:

> In 1930 only 3 million Americans couldn't read. Most of the 1 million white illiterates and the 2 million black illiterates were people over the age of fifty who had never been to school. By 1990, 30 to 35 million U.S. citizens could not read. Most are people under fifty who have been to school for at least eight years. True U.S. literacy figures for adults over 25 have dropped from a 1950 high of 98 per cent to a 1990 low of 81 to 83 per cent. Seventy nations have higher literacy percentages.[6]

Dr. Siegfried Engelmann of the University of Oregon has this to say in his book *War Against the School's Academic Child Abuse*:

> The person who may be most responsible for the whole-language movement in the U.S. is Kenneth Goodman, past president of the International Reading Association. Goodman has been around for years, using his conception of linguistics to pose as an advocate for the underdog—the disadvantaged, the non-English speaker. He and his wife, Yetta, wrote a paper, "Twenty Questions about Teaching Language" that is often quoted by whole-language advocates. I believe that their response to this paper shows that whole-language advocates are not very critical readers. Here's an example from the Goodmans:
>
> > Early in our miscue research, we concluded that a story is easier to read than a page, a

> page easier than a paragraph, a paragraph eas-
> ier than a sentence, a sentence easier than a
> word, and a word easier than a letter.

Our research continues to support this conclusion
and we believe it to be true. How could the kid read
a sentence without being able to read the component
words? If the words are harder than the sentences,
and if the sentences are composed of words, what
phenomenal kind of linguistic gymnastics permits
the kids to transcend the more difficult unit (words)
to get to the easier unit (sentences)?

Most of us know how hard it is for a kid to
"read" a letter like B or J; the Goodmans assert that it
is much, much easier for the kid to read a story. If
something is harder than something else, there's a
greater probability that somebody would fail to learn
it. If the Goodman "hierarchy" of difficulty is accurate, we would expect to find some kids would flu-
ently and accurately read stories, but when asked to
read a page, they would tend to make more mistakes.
These kids would stumble miserably over individual
words and would have incredible trouble following
directions to identify individual letters. I've seen lots
of kids who have reading problems, but never one
with the "Goodman syndrome." Have you?[7]

This is the kind of edu-babble behind the whole-language
learning method. One student recently tested in the second
percentile in reading. This young man was the son of a doctor and had what was considered a normal life. He was
labeled by the school with an attention deficit disorder and

dyslexia. He was consigned to a special program. The parent, however, provided study in phonics and intense direct approach learning. After one year of being presented with this method for forty-five minutes each day, that same child tested in the sixty-first percentile.

KIDS LABELED DYSLEXIC CAN DO WELL

The numbers of children being labeled and written off as developmentally disabled or dyslexic is tragic. It doesn't have to be. It's reprehensible on the part of those who do this to kids, refusing to take any responsibility. The disheartened parent is left not knowing where to turn or what to do. The fact is that when taught properly, with self-discipline, nearly all children can excel.

Phonics, on the other hand, causes children to learn the relationship between the letters of our alphabet and the sound of those letters as we speak them. The purpose isn't for kids to recite the formula for letters and sounds, but for them to understand that there is a constant that can be relied upon (variations of the sounds are included). Once this is learned a young child can tackle all kinds of words. With this basic foundational knowledge, many children have taught themselves to read far beyond their contemporaries.

There are variations in teaching phonics, but this is the basic approach. Organizations promoting phonics have voluminous material showing the power and success of this method. Many older children have failed to learn to read because all they were ever exposed to was look-say, whole-language reading.

Many children unable to learn under the whole-language method become labeled with all manner of learning disabilities by the education establishment. Always the parents' fault, the student's fault, the crowded conditions, but never, ever is the method called into question. Thankfully there are schools and individuals who will take these disabled kids and teach them to read with phonics. As if by magic their disability almost always goes away.

Over and over again the reading scores of private and home school children are overwhelmingly superior to public school children. Nearly all home schools and most private schools are committed to intensive phonics as the foundation for learning how to read well. Admittedly, this isn't the only reason reading scores are better, but can it be reasonably denied as a major contributing factor?

PROJECT FOLLOW THROUGH

The debate over teaching methodology continues… sometimes in the face of the facts. From 1968 to 1977 the federal government conducted what may be the largest educational study ever to take place. It was named *Project Follow Through*. The U.S. Office of Education spent one billion of your tax dollars to make a definitive comparison between teaching methods.[8] Nearly the entire spectrum of teaching methods was represented: from direct instruction to open education. For our purposes it isn't important to know the differences between all the methods represented on the charts below. It is enough to know that the direct instructional method is a phonics-intensive method, while the Tucson Early Education model is essentially identical to the whole-language approach.

AFFECTIVE SELF-ESTEEM

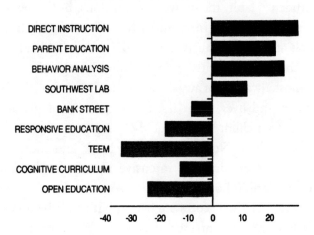

LANGUAGE

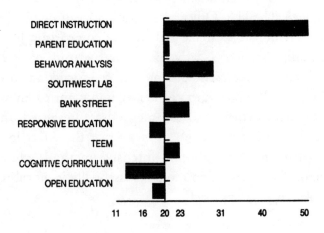

TOTAL MATH

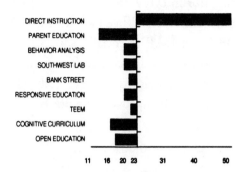

TOTAL SPELLING

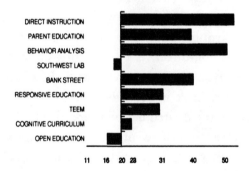

TOTAL READING

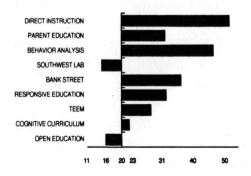

This research, demonstrating that the direct instruction method is superior in every category of teaching, is from the federal government's own Office of Education. By what they advocate, OBE and DAP essentially contradict this research in total. Sometimes it is difficult to let our favorite theories go, but when clear superiority can be established, it is time to embrace what has been proven to work best.

THE NEW CLASSROOM: GRADES FOUR THROUGH TWELVE

In the disorganization of the OBE primary classroom, the need for someone to "keep the lid on" is readily apparent. At least there is something for the facilitator to do. In the higher grades, the role of the facilitator changes from being the trouble-shooter to something less certain. The facilitator is non-directive. Of necessity, students will learn at their own pace. OBE does away with the time-based assessment so it doesn't matter how long it takes a student to demonstrate the desired behavior or attitude change.

In a classroom of twenty students, there could conceivably be twenty different levels of learning occurring at the same time, at least until the top students finished and became tutors for slower students. How do you assess so diverse a class? Before the advent of personal computers, it would have been nearly impossible to manage such an unwieldy task. The computer plays a major role, solving many logistical problems in OBE management and assessment—the subject of chapter six.

1. Ron Brandt, "A Conversation with Bill Spady," *Educational Leadership*, December 1992/January 1993.
2. This list appears in the guidelines for implementing

Oregon H.B. 3565, "Non-Graded Primary," *Task Force Report,* Oregon Department of Education, Salem, Oregon, January 1993, 5-6.

3. Ibid.

4. Ibid.

5. Gladys Hunt, *Honey for a Child's Heart* (Grand Rapids, Michigan: Zondervan, 1989).

6. *National Review,* September 1992, 52.

7. Siegfried Engelmann, *War Against the Schools' Academic Child Abuse* (Portland, Ore.: Halcyon House, 1992) 30.

8. For further information on *Project Follow Through,* see *Harvard Educational Journal,* vol. 46, November 1977; "The Oregon Direct Instruction Model, Comparative Results in Project Follow Through," University of Oregon Follow Through Project, May 1977; *War Against the School's Academic Child Abuse,* by Siegfried Engelmann, Halcyon Press, 1992.

CHAPTER SIX

Managing and Assessing the Students

anaging the OBE classroom will be no easy matter. In fact it would be impossible without a computer. With students doing different projects some of the time and being at different levels of competency on common projects, managing their activity becomes a gargantuan task. The use of personal computers, however, can simplify this process.

Transformational OBE necessitates that each student work at a computer monitor. The teacher will step farther away from involvement with the student as the computer assumes the role of facilitator. There are two management tools that will enable the teacher and computer to work together. One is called a working portfolio (for the teacher), and the other is called the electronic portfolio (for the computer).

From the time a student enters school, information about that student is collected in two ways. First is the working portfolio where students select what they believe is representative of their best work. Second is the electronic portfolio. This information bank includes an astounding array of personal details. Parents interested in their child's work should ask to see the child's working portfolio. It is here that a child's actual work is contained. Grades may show up, but not failing grades. Working portfolios are the OBE substitute for quizzes, tests, and grades.

The electronic portfolio is presently being implemented in some areas. You will hear that schools near you don't have any such thing, and that may well be the case. Remember that implementing OBE is done in stages—slowly, with patient gradualism. In Oregon, it is just beginning. This electronic portfolio will set up a file on each child. In the file will be the history of the child's relationship to the learning outcomes.

These computer files become the basis upon which the school will determine remediation requirements for each student. Remember, remediation is the process of sending students back through the information to give them another chance to demonstrate that they have assimilated the desired behavior or attitude required for a given outcome, such as understanding diversity or deliberation of public issues.

The electronic portfolio will also include medical records, psychological data, personal and family data, and any disciplinary action or confrontations. This information is to be made available to other state agencies and to the employer after graduation.

NO MORE CONTROL OVER PERSONAL RESUMÉ

Some argue that most of this kind of information is available right now so what's the big deal. Don't be taken in.

The information that currently exists on an individual is not accessible from one government agency to another without the consent of that person. Furthermore, individuals control what information is used in their resumé. If Johnny had a bad year or a personality conflict with a teacher, he has the opportunity and the right to determine what information to include and what to leave out of a resumé. He can present himself with his best foot forward.

Not so with the OBE portfolio. It takes away the option of keeping personal information personal. This electronic file will follow Johnny throughout his life.

Students' right to privacy is a thing of the past with files like this, not to mention the rights and the privacy of the mother and father. The following questions were taken from the kinds of tests designed to provide information for the electronic portfolio:

1. I care what my parents think about the things that I do. (Y/N)
2. I love my parents. (Y/N)
3. When you have sex, how often do you and/or your partner use a birth control method such as birth control pills, a condom (rubber), foam, diaphragm, or IUD? (multi-choice)
4. I respect my father and mother. (Y/N)
5. I believe that tithing (giving 1/10 of one's earnings to the church) is one's duty to God. (Y/N)
6. I am an important member of my family. (Y/N)
7. How many really close friends your age do you have? (multi-choice)
8. My parents expect too much of me. (Y/N)

9. I have pretty eyes.(Y/N)
10. During the week how many hours do you attend services, groups, or programs at a church or synagogue? (multi-choice)
11. I like being the way I am. (Y/N)
12. My family life is happy. (multi-choice)
13. People pick on me. (Y/N)
14. How many times in the last month have you had a good conversation with one of your parents that lasted 10 minutes or more? (multi-choice)
15. I am picked on at home. (Y/N)
16. In the last year, how often, if at all, have you thought about killing yourself? (multi-choice)
17. There is a lot of love in my family. (Y/N)
18. It is against my values to have sex while I am a teenager. (multi-choice)
19. Children have a duty to obey their parents at all times. (multi-choice)[1]

On one test, nine out of one hundred questions asked about personal religious beliefs and practice.[2] These are real questions from tests that have already been given. One might complain that this list isn't a representative sample because it doesn't include any academic questions. There is a simple rejoinder to this challenge. The four tests these questions were taken from contained a total of 347 questions, but not one of those questions was academic in any way. Is this the kind of information you want the state to collect from your son or daughter in school?

To protect students from this type of invasive testing the federal Hatch Amendment was passed in the mid 1970s as *The Protection of Pupil Rights Act.* Essentially the act declares that no student shall be required to submit to psychological testing or psychiatric treatment to elicit information in the following areas:

- sexual behavior and attitudes
- mental and psychological problems
- illegal, anti-social, self incriminating or demeaning behavior
- critical appraisals of family members
- privileged relationships (lawyers, physicians and ministers)
- political affiliations
- income
- various other forms of self-incriminating evidence

This law prohibits the use of federal money for the psychological testing of children. However, psychological testing has become very common. From Oregon alone I have collected numerous psychological tests from schools. What happened to the teeth of the Hatch Amendment? Educational bureaucrats have taken an end run around parents. When challenged with the law against such tests, the state can argue that there is no federal money involved. The federal government gives the money to the state. The state then gives money to the district. The district administers the test. The federal money stopped at the state coffers. Therefore, there is no protection for students under the *Protection of Pupil Rights Act*. (For a way to change this in your state see appendix three.)

PSYCHOLOGICAL TESTING OF CHILDREN WILL CONTINUE

When I personally inquired about this violation of federal law, I was given the same story—it could not be established that this test was connected to any federal funds, therefore it was not a violation of the law. I then took one of the tests to our legislative counsel to ask if she felt this was a violation. She stated, "This is a violation of the Hatch Amendment." It is only a matter of time before school districts lose millions of dollars in court battles for violating the rights of students. Parents in several states are pursuing lawsuits to defend their children.

Every year bits of information are added to the student portfolio right up through receiving a certificate of initial mastery and then a certificate of advanced mastery. Before long a solid grasp of who individual students are, how they think, what they believe, and what they value is readily available to anyone with access to the portfolios.

Consider the following statement of two OBE proponents that appeared in *Education Leadership* magazine:

> The computer...is ideally suited to the role of *facilitator* in values education. It inherently possesses the *Rogerian* qualities of genuineness and congruence.... The computer then formulates *open-ended questions* from key words, which causes the respondent to focus and further clarify feelings. In other words, the computer can assume the role of a *nondirective counselor....Values clarification* and *values analysis* are aptly suited to being used as a basis for software development...the computer's vast storage capacity permits access to a much broader base of data than just one classroom. In fact, the responses of the entire population of a school system could easily be compiled, stored, and shared (emphasis added).[3]

In other words, "We can control a lot of people with the computer." *Education Leadership* is not some obscure magazine. It is a trade journal for education in this country. Motives notwithstanding, this incredible advance in education technology can be used for good or ill. But shouldn't someone stop and ask, Do we want large banks of student-specific, personal information collected throughout our children's educational experience? Surely the answer is a resounding no! This is a recipe for abuse and control. And it is not merely a potential development that we can anticipate. It is here today. Consider another statement that outlines how portfolio information will be made available:

> Another area of potential development in computer applications is the attitude changing machine.... For instance, *after first determining a student's constellation of attitudes through appropriate testing procedures, the machine would calculate which of these are amenable to change.*

> There is considerable evidence that such techniques do effectively change attitudes. The question again arises, what is the appropriate subject material (or "attitudes" in this instance) with which to indoctrinate the student?... A psychological research program is underway to study the problems of training a student in decision-making skills.... Does the educator know what values to attach to the different outcomes of these decisions?... *What about students whose values are out of line with the acceptable values of democratic society? Should they be taught to conform to someone else's accepted judgement or proper values?*

Training in decision-making is ultimately com-
pounded with *training in value judgment* and, as
such, becomes a controversial subject that *needs to be
resolved by educators* before the tools can be put to use
(emphasis added).[4]

AM I TO UNDERSTAND THAT OBE CALLS FOR THE STATE TO
COLLECT PERSONAL DATA ON MY SON AND DAUGHTER?

Quite right. In effect, after your children's values are
identified and assessed, the specially programmed computer
will go to work to change your children's convictions and
values to make them conform to a pre-determined standard.
This is clear, unabashed brainwashing. This blatant admission of the goal of shaping the attitudes and behaviors of our
children's character should be sending parents into orbit. Is
this what you send your kids to school for? Are you willing
to have your children's attitudes and values evaluated by a
pre-programmed computer? Who is programming the computers? From what perspective is the software developed?

This is not a Democrat or Republican issue, this is not a
liberal or conservative issue. The OBE paradigm is bad for
America. It provides whoever controls government with the
power (information), the mechanism (education), and the
tools (student-specific portfolio and computer values training) to control behavior.

The innate subjectivity of OBE assessment invites abuse.
For example the following outcome is commonly found
throughout the U.S.:

Communicate: Communicate through reading, writing, and listening.

This outcome is nebulous, inviting a broad, subjective interpretation. The teacher then receives the instruction: Record/evaluate "natural progression of skills within the context of a meaningful whole." What does this mean? What, then, does the child actually do? The student's response is subjective, and so is the teacher's (facilitator's) evaluation. There is not one element of objectivity. This is one of the main problems with OBE assessment. Few parents believe it is just for their children to be exposed to the whims of a subjective evaluation.

The California Learning Assessment System (CLAS), at a cost of $55 million, has been implemented. California Department of Education documents inform us that, "CLAS intends to do away with tests that measure knowledge gains." Rather, CLAS will evaluate "the students' ability to construct meaning."

So how does this play out? Here is the given example: The eighth-grade reading CLAS test provides a sample text for the student to read. At this time the students are 'invited' to share their thoughts and feelings on the text. Nothing more is required. No grammatical standards, no content evaluation, no reasoning, nothing more than feelings. The eighth-grade students are not even required to write their feelings because the test provides a large drawing of an empty head (open mind) to fill with doodlings.[5]

How can the education establishment be so far away from what parents want for their children? They simply have a different agenda and they are going to pursue it. With the subjectivity innate in any system that "intends to do away with tests that measure knowledge gains," abuse can't be far away.

In OBE, academic achievement and striving for excellence have been supplanted by a new value: equality. It is the key requirement and continuing goal replete in OBE literature. This is part of the reason why the system moves away from assessing knowledge acquisition and assimilation. The ideas of honor roll, valedictorian, talented and gifted, and special education are out. All students will reach for the same outcomes or performance objectives. Some will get there sooner, but they will tutor the slower students. It would be an assault on the slower learner's self-esteem should there be discrimination in student treatment and designation.

Parents are concerned about how their children are learning. Are they average, excelling, or learning slowly? Even in the later grades, parents care about how well their children read. Not only are moms and dads interested in specific subjects, but they are also concerned about their children's personal growth and interaction with others. There is so much that is important for parents to be abreast of as children progress through school. It is important for parents to know where to encourage, where to build-up, and what areas to steer kids away from for their own good. There may be a few parents who don't do a good job at this sort of thing. And there are even some parents who don't care and do nothing. The greatest percentage of American parents, however, care a great deal about their kids' education and future. Unless parental care transforms into parental action the slide away from academic rigor will continue.

Recently a father observed that his nine-year-old daughter didn't seem to be able to read at all. She brought home very little homework, and when she did, she wasn't doing the work. Finally he told her to go upstairs and do her homework. About fifteen minutes later, she came back down in tears, claiming she couldn't do the assignment without her group. OBE had trained this girl to believe that she could only accomplish things collectively.

The father was shocked at such a statement from his daughter. He and his wife were anxious to meet with their daughter's teacher. At the conference they were given no information about their daughter's abilities, progress, weaknesses, or strengths. They found the report card had been so changed that they could not conclude anything helpful about where their little girl stood. The teacher answered direct questions by saying, "Your daughter is where she should be, for her." Any discussion of poor performance in a subject such as reading was met with a concern of not hurting the child's self-esteem and with the response, "She is where she is comfortable for her."

The father, having observed his daughter's inability to read, was very upset. The daughter was called in, and she and the teacher went through the girl's portfolio. In this working portfolio were a few pictures drawn by the girl, some paste-up book reports, and some cubes colored red. There were no tests, no written reports. This work represented an entire reporting period. The parents were appalled. They have now made plans which require extreme financial sacrifice on their part. Their child is in private school.

The traditional report card lists each subject followed by a grade. This grade, regardless of whether it is a letter or number, has relevance to the norm. The norm enables parents and educators to measure excellence, diligence, and discipline, or weakness, failure, bad attitudes, and potential learning disabilities. One can also measure progress over the cumulative reporting periods. These grades are relevant to the subject and what the child has learned in relation to what the teacher has taught, which is also measurable.

GRADES HAVE NO MEANING

Another OBE mantra is that grades don't mean anything. In every circle of teachers I have spoken to on this subject the same position is voiced. It's another knee-jerk reaction to the doctor's rubber hammer. If it is currently true that grades don't mean anything it is only because they have been stripped of their meaning. When teachers give grades higher than the student actually deserves, this devalues the grade. If a child develops a bad attitude, refuses to do the class work or assignments, and fails the test, that student has earned an F for fail. The fruit of that child's labor is an F. The F is that student's property. If a teacher instead gives a D, the teacher is both stealing that child's property and lying to that child as well.

There are some children who struggle because of the particular circumstances that life currently has them in. To have someone lie to them about their achievement on top of the troubles they bring to school is truly uncaring. The self-esteem of struggling students isn't enhanced by having an adult lie to them about their achievement. When students have a clear picture of where they are and then are helped and encouraged to do better, just watch the self-esteem soar.

Grades are a positive tool that help the student know where they are academically. An F doesn't mean someone is a bad person. Such a grade only reveals where that student must make an extra effort to improve. The only way a grade will damage self-esteem is if the giving of it is mishandled by someone who lacks professionalism and doesn't recognize the role of teacher as sacred.

Out in the real world, life is a lot tougher. In the real world students don't get something for nothing. No one gives phoney grades. After graduation, on the job, if one does F quality work, that is the basis on which one will be rewarded. Giving kids bogus grades they haven't earned is a terrible disservice to them. This practice does nothing to prepare students for life after school.

Report cards from the first three stages of the OBE system include the grades A, B, or I (incomplete—this grade does not affect the grade point average). Samples from most of the states are about the same. There is nothing which shows relevance to the course of study. Then there is no way for a parent to evaluate where a child is in relation to a subject, or in relation to what a teacher is supposed to be conveying to the students.

Are we ready to give up grade point averages, honor rolls, valedictorians, and the National Honor Society all in the name of equality? If this sounds like a socialistic system, it is. But students are not equal. Everyone is unique. OBE shoves each student through an educational sausage-maker and ignores individual differences. Are you willing to continue year after year of not knowing how your children are measuring up, where your children excel, what your children are capable of, or what bad habits they have developed that need to be corrected?

In some way or another we have all been tested. Testing has always been a part of learning. It is an integral part of the process of demonstrating knowledge, information, and skills. But in transformational OBE, all objective standards for testing are eliminated.

WITH OBE, TESTING LOSES ITS RELEVANCE

OBE is supposed to do away with the idea of a time-based education. This means that it doesn't matter how long it takes a student to demonstrate mastery of an outcome. The way this will be accomplished is by the process of continual remediation. A student will continually be taken through the material until mastery is demonstrated. Tests will be taken over and over again until the student "gets it."

If children are allowed to take and re-take the same test until they get an A or some variation of that grade, what has been measured? What has been accomplished? Yes, those students now have the same grade as the ones who passed the test the first or second time and we have created equality, but what has really been achieved? Taken enough times, a test can be passed simply through trial and error. Top students respond, "Why bother? We all get the same grade anyway." The slower students or the ones with bad attitudes say, "Why bother? I can take it again later."

The effect of not holding students to a measurable, time-based standard is disastrous—especially during the years when they are developing study habits. It is axiomatic that study habits don't come naturally to the majority of students. The critical nature of study habits is that they become our work habits. If students don't learn the discipline of accuracy, deadlines, and accountability in the educational environment, they are ill-prepared for the workplace.

This system encourages the worst impulses of students, taking them further and further away from real achievement. To reach their greatest potential, students must be held to high, demanding standards. OBE assessment exacerbates this trend. Its inherent subjectivity—the very nature of OBE—

invites abuse. The psychological testing that OBE relies upon to determine what students' attitudes are is an extreme invasion of privacy. It is thoroughly inappropriate for the state to collect and keep electronic records of student attitudes, beliefs, and medical status. Only by confining the testing of students to academic subjects will their rights be protected.

If students pass the assessment at the tenth grade, they will be awarded the CIM-certificate of initial mastery. After completing the next two years they will receive the CAM-certificate of advanced mastery. We'll discuss these subjects in chapter seven.

1. These tests included "Wellness and Me: A portfolio project for lifetime health," given to high school students at Lake Ridge High, Lake Oswego, Oregon, September 1993; "Confucius Say," given to fourth through eighth graders at the Pinehurst School, Ashland, Oregon, March 1994; "Attitudes and Behaviors," from the Search Institute Profiles of Student Life; and an unnamed test given in 1993 to fifth and sixth graders at Kelly Creek School in Gresham, Oregon.

2. "Wellness and Me: Portfolio project for lifetime health."

3. Joseph A. Braun Jr. and Durt A. Slobodzian, *Education Leadership,* April 1982.

4. Don D. Bushnell, "The Role of the Computer in Future Instructional Systems," *Instructional Systems AN Communication Review,* March/April 1963.

5. Michelle Malkin, *FWR Report,* October 1993, 7.

CHAPTER SEVEN

CIM, CAM, College and Business

N ot all states are using mastery certificates at this point. Yet they are an important part of what outcome-based education is. The actual implementation of the highest form of OBE, transformational OBE, requires certificates of mastery. The first certificate is normally attained at about age fifteen or sixteen, at approximately the tenth grade level. At this juncture students select material from their portfolios which they will present to a panel in order to demonstrate why they should receive their CIM. Perhaps they will choose a poem, a piece of art, or a speech, or some other such project from their portfolios. When these are accepted, students qualify for the mastery certificate. After the CIM is received, what were juniors and seniors will now be involved in strands (areas of interest for their careers). Some students will be able to continue on toward college, but the vast majority will be directed to vocational training. After two years or more in a particular strand, students will receive the advanced mastery certificate and be ready for the job market.

ISN'T FIFTEEN YEARS OLD TOO YOUNG TO MAKE A CAREER DECISION?

Most people believe no one should be forced to make a career decision at any age. This is a personal decision. Consider typical first- or second-year college students. How many times do these students change their major before settling on a career? In most states, kids will be able to change strands—but only if there is room and, more importantly, if they can get permission. The Oregon labor commissioner has stated publicly, "These strands will be very competitive." If that is so, it will be even more difficult for someone to change.

The idea of big business being able to work with the school to ease the young person into the world of employment has merit. If a student has learned the basics well there are real advantages to seeing and working first-hand with cutting edge technology.

But even if the OBE system had been designed to teach the basics well, there would still be severe logistical problems if kids are to be given an equal chance in this system of early vocational training. What about the students who live in the tiny rural community that has a few stores surrounded by farms or some other limited industry. How will the schools satisfy the requirement? Will their students have to leave home for the area that offers technology training before they reach eighteen?

DOESN'T VOCATIONAL TRAINING HAVE SOME MERIT?

Absolutely. The concept of vocational training is an excellent one. Many young people will not go to college. This is why the community college system is not only important but essential. The increase in support to community and vocational colleges is critical. The fact that the community college system is so successful is further evidence of the lack of necessity to change the entire system of primary and secondary education in this country.

WILL COLLEGES ACCEPT MY KID'S CAM?

In Oregon many schools of higher education, concerned about their own academic reputation, have said that the subjective CAM and portfolios won't replace SAT scores and grade point averages. It is easy to foresee the problem of children who haven't received a solid education in kindergarten through twelfth grade attempting to get into a good college only to discover they do not possess the knowledge required to score high enough on their SAT or other college entrance exams. The best colleges and universities may come to accept the CAM designation, but how long will it take and how many colleges and universities will make the change?

ARE THE INTERESTS OF BUSINESS AND EDUCATION SYNONYMOUS?

The entire business community in this country is looking for ways to pick up the quality of this nation's work force. No one can deny the country's need for better-skilled, better-trained workers. Industries exhaust themselves to stay on the cutting edge of the new technology. They have a right to look for and even expect employees who can keep up with the modern, fast-paced business world. The business community is disappointed with the quality of worker who arrives on the scene from school. Their inability to read well or at all, to spell, add, and subtract are legitimate problems. The horror stories are abundant in every state. There is a new interest in education by the business world, and that is a good thing.

The proper direction and use of that interest is imperative, however. If business is looking anew at education to rebuild an unstable economy, meet higher productivity, and create a work force that will compete in the world marketplace, fair enough. But don't ever forget the following maxim: Business is about profits and kindergarten through twelfth grade is about students.

This is a difference that was overlooked in the SCANS report which refers to children as "human resource material." There is a serious question to be considered: What is the motive in the attempt by business to reshape education? Does big business really have the individual's value in mind? Yes, if one is talking about the individual's value to business. The goal, as previously stated by proponents, is to ensure a massive work force that will compete with third world countries for labor and factory type jobs.

Don't misunderstand. I am a strong defender of business and business profits—the more, the better. But let's not forget, business is business and the business of business is profit. This is the first priority, as it should be. The purpose of this renewed interest in education is not driven by a desire to create a system that will provide superior academic achievement and the development of broad-based skills that will allow the individual flexibility of choice in careers throughout life. How does requiring students at age fifteen or sixteen to make career choices and then training those children in that narrow area of interest have their best interests in mind? Is business going to become the customer of education for business' needs, or will parents be the customer of education for their children's lifelong aspirations?

The work-school concept is closely tied to outcome-based education in education reform, but it doesn't need to be and it shouldn't be—not in the first through the twelfth grade. Implementing a system based on similar fallacious thinking in England created a crisis. The system that started out sending some kids to trade school and work transition and a few selected students on to college worked to further entrench the class system. A few went on to college, but most never received the opportunity to go on. They also lost their lateral mobility. The great increase in unemployment and crime was laid at the feet of the system of education, and England has recently abandoned this approach as a complete failure.

It isn't necessary to change our entire nation's system of education to accomplish a smooth transition from school to work. In the early 1960s such transition programs, called distributive education or variations of that name, were abundant. The student would spend half or part of a day in school and the other half or part on the job. Here the teacher coordinated closely with the employer. The employer's evaluation of the student's job performance became a part of the student's grade for the class.

Once again, I am unwaveringly committed to the support of business and profits and the entire free enterprise system. We mustn't, however, confuse the goal of business with the goal of primary and secondary education. They can be compatible, but they are most certainly not synonymous.

There are other problems with the OBE system of mastery.

It has been suggested that no one will be hired into the work force without obtaining a certificate of mastery. But the CIM isn't obtainable without demonstrating the desired behaviors and outcomes. Since OBE is so much involved with the affective side of education, it's conceivable that students must demonstrate the proper attitudes and behaviors before they can obtain a job.

Does this sound too extreme? A bit alarmist? The original draft of the education reform bill in Oregon called for precisely this kind of control. It did not allow a student to be hired into the job market without having received a certificate of initial mastery. No summer jobs and no weekend jobs during school were allowed. There was significant objection to this and it was changed in the final draft. The subsequent wording was interesting, however. "The proposed rule shall provide opportunities to participate in the employment decision-making relating to the minor, the minor's parents or guardian, local school authorities and the potential employer."

It appears that the only thing that changed was that the school wormed its way into the process. So now kids can work, but only if the school approves of the job. With this kind of precedent, it's not hard to believe that such an outrageous thing as "no certificate, no job" is possible on a national level.

The OBE system is being designed for maximum control. This is the type of abuse that increasing government control invites. The restrictions that appeared in the original Oregon bill didn't get there by the slip of a pen. People who believe the government should control the lives of students were testing the water, seeing how far they could go—this time. Government has little capacity to restrain itself. Only when people stand against such invasions will freedom be retained.

MINORITIES SUSPECT OBE OF RACISM

Minorities have expressed serious objections to OBE as well. They recognize the insidious nature of a system that will direct most of them into training for vocations rather than allowing them to work toward a broad-based education and greater opportunity. Speaking of Oregon's OBE bill, H.B. 3565, African American, Hank Sanders, who currently an Alabama State Senator, said:

> I see this bill as a fraud...What they have done is taken tracking and repackaged it.[1]

Sanders defines "tracking" as an informal filtering system within schools. The result is that many Blacks are directed into specific vocational, non-academic areas as opposed to receiving a broad-based education.

ACADEMIC RHETORIC VS. EDUCATIONAL REALITY

Most of the laws across the country dealing with the implementation of OBE at any level have the phrase "world class education" or "rigorous intellectual standards," or even "best educated citizens in the world by the year 2000." These phrases seem to be little more than the carefully chosen rhetoric of the promoters and marketing machine behind OBE. In reality, across the nation, the major complaint of parents and parent groups is that OBE has lowered academic standards everywhere it has been tried.

In Oregon, the Department of Education has published what it calls task force recommendations which came from task forces designed to make written recommendations of how OBE would be implemented on a state-wide basis. In Oregon's certificate of initial mastery are recommendations for tenth grade achievement in math. Here is an example: "Brainstorm a list of all of the energy transformations involved in taking a shower. Be careful to consider everything that is required to take a shower." In layperson's language, here are the content goals for math after ten years of study. These goals were published January 14, 1994:

- about numbers and what they mean
- to measure and weigh things by using numbers
- to gather and organize numbers to communicate with others
- to add, subtract, multiply, and divide numbers and when to do each
- to use numbers and patterns to understand and explain our world
- to use numbers to talk about shapes and spaces

This, after 10 years of math. No wonder parents are offended and angry. This is not a credible attempt at academic excellence. Perhaps fourth grade students would benefit from curriculum that ended with such a test question but certainly not students in the tenth grade. It's outrageous, and unfortunately it is not an isolated case. The rhetoric of excellence accompanied by lower standards is found in every state that has tried OBE. The long history of rejection and failure of OBE is the subject of chapter eight.

1. "Katz Plan on Schools Given 'F' by Activists," *the Oregonian*, Metro NW, Saturday, 4 May 1991.

The Failure/Rejection of OBE–Everywhere

G ood schools have been tragically struck by OBE. Ballard High School in eastern Jefferson County, Kentucky, was just such a school. Ballard was not merely good. A tradition of genuine excellence in education had persisted in this school year after year. Here were teachers and students in honest pursuit of academic excellence. Ballard High School students maintained such high levels of achievement they were held up as national examples of academic quality—setting the standard for others to follow. Parents and students had a reason to be proud. Ballard students consistently scored well above the average on the SAT and ACT tests. Fully ninety-five percent of Ballard graduates went on to college. In 1993 this school had twenty-one National Merit semi-finalists. Ballard High School's academic standards were second to none.

Then a grey haze settled over the administration at Ballard. As Kentucky began to implement outcome-based education, a new assessment tool was developed—a state-wide exam which now tests the new kind of education, the OBE way of learning. By now you will anticipate that this new test de-emphasized academic knowledge gain. A strange phenomenon occurred when the state administered this new assessment test to Ballard High students. The failure rate was phenomenal.

The teaching staff, parents, and students were shocked. How could the top Ballard students have done so poorly on a standardized test? The results were so bad that Ballard High was placed under evaluation with the potential of being declared "a school in crisis" (another OBE designation that paves the way for taking control away from local administrators). Here, where academic excellence and independent thinking flourished, the students are now designated "at risk." This is a school that has a long history of sending students to Ivy League colleges. The intrusion into Ballard's system would be laughable if it weren't so disgusting.

How did this happen? The reason is clear. The excellent Ballard students had been taught the importance of thinking for themselves. They had focused on true learning and academic scholarship. These students had not yet been socialized and indoctrinated to exhibit "appropriate" attitudes and behaviors. Unlike Pavlov's dogs, the top-notch Ballard students, to their credit, didn't respond on cue. Any system of education that takes high achievers and makes failures out of them is dangerous, indeed.

OBE is a bad experiment spawned by a collectivist philosophy that hurts the students it is allowed to touch. Read the warning signs. Those who care about students' academic achievement and potential for fulfillment in life must unite to stand against the rising tide of educational destruction driven by social planners.

IS MORE TIME NEEDED?

OBE proponents across the land continue to ask for a little more time to sort out the short falls and fine tune the system. "Give it chance to work," is the cry. The standard time allotment for active implementation of OBE is five years. In essence this time frame gives those pushing OBE a hiatus from evaluation of what they are doing. But after five years of active implementation, OBE will be so inculcated into the system that it would be a colossal task to back away from it. Some speculate this is the precise reason five years is sought for implementation.

Any system that asks parents to expose their children to dramatic philosophical and methodology change, ought to be able to supply reams of empirical research data to establish the academic improvement that can be expected for the children by this change. Yet there is none. Parents are asked to consider theory and potentials and then wait five years to evaluate what has happened. There is another reason OBE advocates want more time before what they have done is evaluated. There is no example of success in raising academic scores as a result of implementing outcome-based education. Not one! The record of attempts and resultant failures or rejections of OBE is long. There is no need to embellish it. This is the public record of OBE.

MAINE

After mastery learning, scores were lower than projected (average was 250; projection was between 300 and 350).

ARIZONA

The Arizona legislature turned down OBE. The Arizona

Federation of Teachers is opposed to Skinnerian techniques. They killed the bill in committee.

VIRGINIA

"Governor Wilder has heard the outcry of Virginians about the dangerous direction that education reform had taken, and he has acted. Yesterday afternoon he axed Outcome-Based Education." So reports the *Richmond Times Dispatch*, September 16, 1993. Virginian parents were against what was happening to their children and academic standards in their state. Through concerted effort they got this reform stopped statewide.

COLORADO

According to the November 18, 1993, *Wall Street Journal,* parents' concern about the academic faltering of their students was so great that it actually affected the outcome of the school board election in Littleton. Those school board members promoting the new education were voted out of office by a margin of two to one. Many Littleton parents were concerned the reform "watered down the curriculum and devalued the importance of factual knowledge." *The Rocky Mountain News* of February 2, 1994, reports that indeed the newly elected school board "killed the new standards," just as they had promised.

TEXAS

According to a September 1993 item in the *Education Reporter,* amid a heavy controversy throughout the election cycle of the Independent School District over mastery learning and OBE, the trustees voted 6-1 to drop OBE from the Goose Creek schools. They cited that mastery learning had been a failure everywhere it has been tried, and the board president observed, "Our product is, or should be, educated children." The board emphasized a "refocus on the instruction of academics" and called for the creation of "verifiable academic graduation standards."

In 1987 San Marco High School in Texas was selected as one of the top high schools in the state, ranking twenty-ninth out of more than eleven hundred schools. Desiring to make a good thing better, San Marco implemented an OBE program in 1990. Two years later, the number of eleventh graders able to pass all sections on a standardized test dropped from 50 percent to 36 percent even though the state average had gone up. "After an intensive six-week study of the OBE literature, we believe it to be a plausible hypothesis that certain aspects of this theory actually generate the negatives you've seen," Joanne Carson, a professor at the University of Texas, testified to the Texas State Board of Education.

IOWA

Statewide education goals dropped. Parents attacked the plan, saying it glossed over basic academic skill and instead attempted to infuse politically correct values into the curriculum.

NEBRASKA

Angry parents in Nebraska appealed to the education leadership to reconsider implementing this new mode. The appeal ended up in the hands of the attorney general, Don Stenberg. The opinion from his office dated Sept. 29, 1993, was direct in its response:

It's clear, it's very clear, that the intent of this bill is simply to say what skills we want young people to have when they come out of school in academic areas. Thus, learner outcomes which are values oriented or which relate to attitudes or which nurture mental health or relate to believing in one's own effectiveness, or taking pride in one's own accomplishments, etc. exceed statutory authority of the Nebraska School Accountability Commission and may not be included.

MICHIGAN

When parents' concerns were continually ignored and scoffed at by the education community, at all levels, their frustration reached its limit. They filed a lawsuit against the State Board of Education. Parents were outraged that 40 percent of the new curriculum dealt with emotional and mental health. The protest became so large the State Senate established a select committee to hear the people. This resulted in a stinging report against the education establishment by the Senate committee.

PENNSYLVANIA

In Pennsylvania the implementation of the vague, broadly interpreted outcomes has been stalled. Pennsylvania's outcomes deal with attitudes and behaviors, not academics. An unstoppable groundswell of angry protest from parents rose to the state legislature and caused a halt to the use of outcomes there. As reported in the *Washington Times* on February 10, 1993, "House Rejects Proposal to Teach Attitudes in School." One representative is quoted as saying, "If they insist on Outcome-Based Education they must come back with outcomes dealing only with academics." The House of Representatives, responding to constituent outcry, rejected the proposal to teach attitudes in the schools. The vote was 139 to 61.

SWEDEN

The above list is only partial in the continuing failure and rejection of OBE around the country. What may be more surprising to people is that OBE-type education is being rejected as a complete failure in other, unexpected places. For years Sweden has been held up as an icon of everything that is good in a progressive society, especially its education system. As of the writing of this book, Oregon's Department of Education guidelines highlight Sweden's education system as one to be emulated. The following excerpt of an article entitled "The Swedish Model" appeared in the *Wall Street Journal,* Tuesday, April 7, 1992:

> Swedish schools have been touted as the most "progressive" in the world, relentlessly pursuing equality at the expense of excellence.
>
> Grades were abolished for students under the age of 15, because they were said to foster competition rather than cooperation among students.
>
> All that is changing under the instruction of Beatrice Ask, Sweden's new 35-year-old education minister. She says that although Sweden spends $7,000 a year per student on education—more than any other country—its young people have only middling scores on comparative international tests and are slipping.
>
> Ms. Ask has a bold reform agenda which begins with

reintroducing grades, requiring that English be taught from the first grade on and encouraging the study of Christian ethics in schools.

Ms. Ask says Americans should think carefully before they follow Sweden's former example and view schools as a center for the delivery of social services. "Swedish schools have diluted the quality of education by trying to do too much," she says. "They may then neglect their basic function—educating children."[1]

In addition to the changes listed in the article, Sweden has implemented a voucher plan what will allow students to go to any school of their choice—private or public. The current batch of education leaders in America have incessantly pointed to Sweden as a model of what education should look like here in the U.S.

The changes that OBE calls for are the very policies that destroyed education in Sweden—the very policies that they have rejected as detrimental to quality education. By what law of logic are the promoters of OBE asking Americans to follow Sweden down the OBE trail at the very time that country is rejecting it as a complete failure...after decades of using it?

ENGLAND

An article in the *Education Reporter*, January 1993, entitled "Progressive Teaching is Rejected in England," describes the fundamental shift occurring in that country. Apparently progressive education was too regressive. After thirty years England is abandoning "progressive" education. It is being replaced with traditional education in specific content-subject areas like math, writing, and history.

FURTHER EVIDENCE OF OBE FAILURE
FROM JOHNS HOPKINS UNIVERSITY

In a study[2] directed by Robert Slavin of Johns Hopkins University, it was concluded that the method of mastery learning (OBE) is, in actuality, a Robin Hood approach taking from the fast learner to help out the poor learner. For "then a common level of learning for all students could only be achieved by taking time away from high achievers to increase it for the low achievers."

In many school districts, parents are complaining that the faster and higher achieving students are being held back. The schools are responding by saying, "No, we wouldn't hold kids back." And parents are believing it. But it is happening. The Johns Hopkins study reveals this flaw in the system, reporting that "students who achieve the criterion early cannot go on to new material, there is a ceiling effect built into the procedure."

Those students experiencing the ceiling effect are made to be peer tutors or receive what is deceptively called horizontal enrichment. Every instance we have researched of horizontal enrichment has been a complete waste of student time. Some peer tutoring is acceptable and may even be helpful, but if high achieving students spend the bulk of their time teaching someone else something they already know, they aren't learning anything new. Parents send their children to school to advance their learning, not to become teachers. When this occurs, "dumbing down education" is the appropriate descriptive phrase.

ARE THERE NO SUCCESS STORIES FOR OBE?

Sweden was the favorite, but of course, it can't be used anymore. There are some alleged successes being held up as examples of OBE. Dr. William Spady often cites a school in New Cannan, Connecticut. This school was supposed to be a positive example of outcome-based education and particularly of outcome-based math. But the school has been closed since the 1983/84 school year. Doesn't is seem odd that proponents of OBE have to go back to 1983 to find what they term a success, a school that didn't make it because of falling enrollment?

One other example of success, OBE style, is to be found in Johnson City, New York. Johnson City has been attempting to make a go of OBE for several years. After $7.5 million was invested, no improvement was seen. Test results stayed flat. The student-teacher ratio was changed to 15 to 1, and teachers spent two weeks each summer in training. Teachers were paid outside their normal contract salary to tutor children.

In this case such a practice would account for the problem of high achieving kids being held back while waiting for or tutoring the slower kids. Still no rising achievement results. With growing desperation the school even changed the test in an attempt to make the system look better. Instead of using standardized tests they have a state regents test. Still the test scores were flat. There has been an immense amount of money and time and effort put into this school, and still the academic success that parents want is eluding them.

Of all the OBE failures, one example is the most poignant. The story is recorded in a report by the Far West Laboratory for Educational Research and Development. William Spady was given a grant from the U.S. Department of Education for developing model schools based on mastery learning and outcome-based education. The first few lines of the conclusion to the grant read as follows:

> The four models of instructional organization outlined in this casebook are difficult programs to implement. The practices of the ten schools described in the case studies are indeed commendable. *Yet we do not offer these ten case studies as "exemplary schools" deserving emulation* (emphasis added).

After the expenditure of countless thousands of your tax dollars, Spady's own research demonstrated OBE to be "not deserving emulation." Today Spady charges ahead with his OBE agenda. It seems that no amount of evidence against OBE, even their own, will dissuade proponents from the social agenda enabled through the implementation of OBE.

A word of caution is in order. Brace yourselves. It won't be long before we will be hearing of new examples of great success all over the nation. Don't be deceived. These success stories will be, generally speaking, from people whose full-time job is to find a way to make OBE look good. As the standards are continually lowered, test scores may look better. Then parents with full-time jobs won't have time to check out all the alleged successes.

Parents only want schools to be safe and for their children to learn a broad base of academic knowledge. That's not asking so much. You would think in view of the continuing record of documented failures in this country and around the world, *someone* in the education community would have the courage to stand up and shout, "It won't work here either!"

It's a disaster that is already damaging kids. Many educators are afraid—afraid for their jobs, for their funding, for their retirement, for their assignments. Some have stood up and faced the loss of their jobs or been reassigned for opposing implementation of OBE. These few have demonstrated their care for their children's future. They are today's heroes.

The real fight has to come from parents and other taxpayers who are fed up with the continual claims of future excellence and the blatant grab for control of the next generation. Those who embrace the idea of government control of education are hard at work. You can hold them at bay, but they will not go away.

1. Reprinted with permission of the *Wall Street Journal,* 1992, Dow Jones and Company, Inc. All rights reserved. For complete text of article, see appendix eight.

2. See Appendix 2 for complete John hopkins University study.

CHAPTER NINE

The Astronomical Cost of a Bad Idea

N o one knows how much OBE will eventually cost. The number may be so high that even if the education community knew the amount they would be hesitant to publish it. There are examples from around the country that reveal some of the costs of implementing various aspects of OBE.

The Kentucky education commissioner proposed to spend $80 million over five years just to test students on the effect of education reform. Remember the new system is driven by outcomes, therefore new testing and assessment tools must be designed. This proposed spending was simply for the cost of designing tests for grades four through eleven.[1]

Oregon's superintendent of public instruction acquired $17 million from Oregon's lottery funds, constitutionally designated for economic development, to use for teacher retraining in OBE. Oregon's law requires the state to develop its own assessment tool. If Kentucky's legislature was asked for $80 million for their assessment tool, it seems reasonable

Oregon's should cost about the same. So Oregonians could be looking at nearly $100 million above their education budget before they even get to the classroom.

- Farnsworth Elementary, in Minnesota, spent $240,552 for 326 students.
- Littleton, Colorado, spent $670,000 for one high school.
- Altogether, Littleton spent $1.3 million for one school district.
- Minnesota spent $40 million for implementation costs.
- Daniel Boone school district in Pennsylvania spent $300,000 for start-up costs.
- The Kentucky legislature was ultimately asked for $500 million for implementation.
- In a June 27, 1991, article in *The Oregonian*, the Oregon Education Association is quoted as estimating it would cost Oregon $2.5 billion to fully implement this new education reform on a state level.
- The country of Sweden spent $7 billion before completely abandoning this system.

Isn't it shocking, considering there is no record of academic success, a long record of failure, and no definitive idea of how much it will cost, that OBE is still not only supported but is actually pushed by the education elite in this country? The real debate is over social agenda. This is why, in full view of abject failure, proponents of OBE can unabashedly push for their cause. Parents of America are being led down a road called education reform that, more and more, resembles a garden path.

1. Lexington *Herald Leader*, 30 July 1991.

Oregon:

A Case Study

I n July 1991, Oregon's House Bill 3565 dealing with education reform was signed by the governor and became law.[1] The previous Speaker of the House, Vera Katz, was chief sponsor and introduced the bill. She is a director of the National Center on Education and the Economy, and she represents Oregon on the New Standards Project. It was through her involvement in these national organizations that Ira Magaziner came to Oregon to tell a special joint session of the House and Senate that Oregon would forge the way in education reform.

The bill passed through the House and Senate easily. I believe most legislators voted for this bill because they hoped that students would finally be required to show mastery of subject material and that academic performance would be improved. Others may have relied on the section of the bill that said it couldn't be implemented without funds, and therefore gave it only cursory scrutiny. As a member of the 1991 Oregon legislature, I am convinced that very few legislators had a thorough understanding of the magnitude of this legislation and what impact it would have on Oregon's education system. In subsequent conversations with many of my colleagues, it would seem few even understand it today.

After the bill passed, the major question left was, Would outcome-based education be implemented in Oregon? Initially, the Department of Education began to tell inquisitive parents that Oregon was not going to do outcome-based education; instead, we were going to do performance-based education. This was quickly challenged by referring to the new law. H.B. 3565 specifically calls for outcomes in Sections 2, 5, and 9.

In a cover letter to a series published by the Department of Education entitled "Toward a National Standard for Oregon's Common Curriculum Goals," our state superintendent of public instruction stated, "They represent the first step toward ensuring that Oregon's curriculum framework can support the development of Outcome-Based Education." Toward the end of her letter, she mentioned Spady and Marshall as encouraging Oregon to move toward outcome-based education. After we shared this information in public meetings around the state, the Department of Education stopped telling people they were not going to implement outcome-based education.

IT PASSED IN '91. WHY BE CONCERNED NOW?

Many have asked, if this bill passed in 1991, why are you just becoming concerned about it in 1994? The reason is quite simple. While we had examined the outcomes and laws passed in other states, it took several months for Oregon's task forces to prepare the plan for implementation and for the Department of Education to publish Oregon's outcomes. As reviewed in an earlier chapter in this book, they were, by and large, dealing with attitudes and behaviors and socialization. It became clear that this new thrust in the direction of education was away from effective education (knowledge-based academic subjects) to affective education dealing with children's attitudes, behaviors, and socialization.

Another concern I had was how specific Oregon's law was regarding outcomes and what would happen if a child was not making satisfactory progress. In Section 21(4) the law states: "If, at any point, a student is not making satisfactory progress toward attainment of the standard at grades 3, 5, 8 and 10, including the Certificates of Initial Mastery and Advanced Mastery, the school district shall make additional services available to the student, that may include but need not be limited to:

(a) A restructured school day;
(b) Additional school days;
(c) Individualized instruction and other alternative instructional practices, and
(d) Family evaluation and social services, as appropriate.

I asked our legislative counsel if this indeed meant that one of the remedies to the school district was to send state social services staff into the home for evaluation of the child's environment. The answer from legislative counsel confirmed my worst suspicions. In presenting this scenario around our state, educators have questioned me from the audience exclaiming, "Do you think we'd ever do something like that?" I have heard various forms of that question, and my answer has always been, "Then why is it even there?"

These are the things that are so caustic to parents; it's a statement that says the children belong to the State, not to the parents. Language like this should never be in a bill. It is not about protection for abused kids as proponents have argued. The language in this section of the bill is not designed for them because it is related directly to the progress in outcomes.

In a further demonstration of the Department of Education's attitude toward parents, our superintendent said in an open debate, "I believe we should grade parents on how they raise kids. I really do." Parents who have called the Department of Education to express concern have been ridiculed for criticizing the reform. Many teachers and superintendents have reported that they dare not raise a word against the reform.

FIVE SPECIFIC AREAS OF CONCERN REGARDING H.B. 3565 IN OREGON.

We will now examine these five concerns in detail: 1) home school and private school, 2) certificates of initial and advanced mastery, 3) site committees and local control, 4) integration of social services, and 5) funding.

HOME SCHOOL AND PRIVATE SCHOOL

The protection of home schools and private schools is a legitimate, major concern to many families in Oregon. Since I know the chair of the house education committee personally, I called to meet with her regarding this issue. In our first personal conversation I asked, "What was the intention of the committee in reference to the outcomes and home schoolers?"

She answered, "The intention is that the outcomes will apply to home schoolers." Two days later she called to inform me that after a further conversation with the Department of Education, she realized the outcomes wouldn't apply to home school. Her final word was "Home school is probably safe."

My concern was not yet satisfied since in several places in the Oregon bill the phrase "all students" appears. I wondered if at some opportune time that might be understood to mean just what it says, *"all students."* I took that concern to legislative counsel; she concurred that it could be easily construed to mean "all students." Upon further discussion, she thought that could be handled with administrative rules by the Department of Education and not even require legislative attention.

CERTIFICATES OF INITIAL MASTERY AND ADVANCED MASTERY

Oregon is leading the country in the elimination of the traditional high school diploma and in implementing the use of the certificate of initial mastery and certificate of advanced mastery. Oregon passed the Education Reform Act in 1991, and in June 1994, students from Cottage Grove High School became the first in the nation to be awarded a certificate of initial mastery.

The following information was acquired from a phone conversation with a parent and community leader from Cottage Grove, Oregon.[2] Cottage Grove began a pilot program to initiate a CIM/CAM program with the freshman class in the 1992/93 school year. First year CIM students are called CIM 1 students, sophomores or second year students are called CIM 2 students. First year CAM students (juniors) are CAM 1, and second year CAM students (seniors) are CAM 2 students. At the beginning of the 1993/94 school year there were approximately 223 sophomores enrolled. By June 1994 there were approximately 183 students still in the program. Roughly 40 students had left. Of those remaining, approximately 105 will receive their CIM in June. Twenty or so will go to summer school to go before a CIM board in August, and twenty or thirty will continue working on their CIM in eleventh grade (will they be called CIM 2.5?). The administration has refused to respond to questions regarding where the students have gone who left school. Did they transfer, drop out, become home schooled, or enroll in private school? Someone knows.

STUDENTS WANT OUT

Student dissatisfaction with the CIM program was so high that 116 students signed a petition requesting they be allowed to drop the CAM program. As a result of the students' petition, it was announced at a parent meeting on June 13, 1994, that for this sophomore class only, a diploma tract will be offered as an alternative to the CAM strands. The number of students who will choose the diploma tract is not known at this time. We should not assume that every student who signed the petition will abandon the CAM route.

Here is a record of the letter written and signed by students on their own initiative to the school board, dated May 20, 1994:

Dear School Board Member,

After two years of the CIM experimentation, at our expense, without clear standards, or measurements, we strongly request that you cease to further experiment with us. We ask that you postpone the installation of the CAM program until the fall of 1996, and only then if you can demonstrate the existence of clear standards, evaluations, and plans for achievement.

Signed,

Students of the Class of 1996

To our knowledge, there has been no official acknowledgement that the letter exists. There is extreme parental concern regarding the success of this program despite constant and repeated communication with school officials. The students have endured extreme experimentation and many are disillusioned.

According to another parent, one CIM 2 student was told two days before the awarding of the CIM certificates that he would not receive his CIM. When he responded that he would transfer to a neighboring school district, he was told that he would not be able to transfer until he completed his IP (in progress) outcome. No transcript would be forwarded until the IP was removed. Another student was told that she would not be able to complete her CAM in two years because of her unsatisfactory progress, despite the fact that she was planning to attend college at the end of her senior year.

Each CIM student spent weeks preparing an oral presentation on why they should receive their CIM. Although there are actually eleven outcomes required to achieve a CIM, the students at Cottage Grove High School were only required to demonstrate seven. With supporting material from their portfolios from the last two years, they were required to demonstrate their proficiency before a board or panel consisting of their block teacher plus three or four other teachers. Family members were invited to attend.

The following requirements are from the Oregon Department of Education, certificate of initial mastery, instructional, learning and assessment system. This is the tool by which the student's presentation is assessed:

FORMS OF REPRESENTATION

- Video production
- Dramatic and Socio-dramatic play
- Creative dramatics

CONCRETE

- Puppetry
- Clay, sand, block construction
- Dance, creative and rhythmic movement
- Music
- Responsive movement
- Counting with objects
- Three-dimensional models, concrete graphs and maps
- Drawing
- Painting
- Collage
- Pictures

TRANSFORMATIONAL

- Pictorial signs
- Pictorial writing
- Gestures
- Tally marks
- Pictorial graphs
- Talk or related expressive forms
- Conventional writing (alphabetic or related expressive forms)

SYMBOLIC/ABSTRACT

- Symbolic paintings
- Mathematics symbols
- Musical notation
- Symbolic signs
- Symbolic graphs and maps

These are the categories in which the Department of Education wants students judged by a panel in order to be awarded the certificate. I wonder by which of these forms of representation they might judge the student's knowledge of math or science or geography? Do you suppose that "responsive movement" or "creative and rhythmic movement" might be used to test these tenth graders as to their knowledge of chemistry or biology?

Looking back at the certificate of initial mastery outcomes for "understanding diversity" required by the Department of Education, I see the requirement to "communicate in a second language." The Department of Education's task force recommendations on the requirements for implementation of the law states:

Extended Outcome Definition:

Second language proficiency has several components that must be considered independently. Using the American Council of Teachers of Foreign Language (ACTFL) framework for second language proficiency, there are five aspects of language proficiency including 1) speaking, 2) listening, 3) reading, 4) writing, and 5) culture. In addition, students will be expected to acquire a deep understanding of one or more cultures that use the target language.

General Performance Expectations:

At the CIM level of performance, students will be able to handle a variety of uncomplicated, basic, and communicative tasks and social situations directed at a sympathetic non-English speaking native speaker. It is also expected that students will demonstrate cultural sensitivity in the communication.

Task Guidelines:

Assessment tasks for this outcome should: (1) go beyond simple needs to include topics related to personal history or leisure time activities; and (2) present a communications problem that needs to be solved which is related to typical person-to-person encounters.

Examples of Tasks: You have a meeting with a non-English speaking client who is interested in purchasing the products your company sells. Be prepared to discuss, in the second language, your product with your client and "sell" your goods using strategies that are appropriate for the target culture. Be prepared to explain, in English, what cultural factors you considered in planning your sales call.

You will be presented with the draft of a letter written in the target language. The letter provides an itinerary for some public officials from another country who will visit your area soon. Edit the letter and prepare a memo in English describing some cultural factors that should be taken into account to help ensure a successful visit.[3]

No doubt when parents read the above requirements of a second language with this degree of proficiency they are totally impressed. But which of the forms of representation would be used to test this very impressive required proficiency: symbolic signs, drawing, puppetry? The point is that none of these "Forms" would test language proficiency. In fact, not one of the students I spoke to had even a rudimentary proficiency, let alone the advanced level described in the rhetoric. If this requirement was waived by the Department of Education for the purpose of awarding the first CIMs in the country, then they are not honest CIMs. The reality of what is actually taking place in the classroom isn't remotely connected to the "world class standards" called for in the law. The parents are being taken in with all the written goals and speeches, but the truth is that it isn't happening. And the great tragedy is that the kids lose out.

After students successfully complete their presentation and are awarded the certificate of initial mastery, they must declare the area of interest (or strand) for advanced study they will focus on for the next phase of their study toward attainment of the certificate of advanced mastery.

Within each endorsement area or strand, there are three slivers (levels of study) consisting of: 1) college bound, 2) community college and/or professional technical study, and 3) preparation for work-force entry. This is very significant because not only are CIM students fifteen or sixteen years old (at about the tenth grade level) required to make a career choice, but they must declare whether they are college bound. (An interesting side note is that after two years of working with this system, most teachers were unaware of the existence of "slivers" and were not familiar with the term when questioned.)

The following are Oregon's six strands, or areas of endorsement, that a student much choose from for the certificate of advanced mastery:

Arts and Communication: Programs of study related to the humanities and to the performing, visual, literary, and medial arts. These may include (but are not limited to) architecture, creative writing, film and cinema studies, fine arts, graphic design and production, journalism, foreign languages, radio/television broadcasting, advertising, and public relations.

Business and Management: Programs of study related to the business environment. These may include (but are not limited to) entrepreneurship, sales, marketing, hospitality and tourism, computer/information systems, finance, accounting, personnel, economics, and management.

Health Services: Programs of study related to the promotion of health as well as the treatment of injuries, conditions and disease. These may include (but are not limited to) medicine, dentistry, nursing, therapy and rehabilitation, nutrition, fitness, and hygiene.

Human Resources: Programs for study related to economic, political, and social systems. These may include (but are not limited to) education, law and legal studies, law enforcement, public administration, child and family services, religion, and social services.

Industrial and Engineering Systems: Programs of study related to the technologies necessary to design, develop, install, or maintain physical systems. These may include (but are not limited to) engineering and related technologies, mechanics and repair, manufacturing technology, precision production, and construction.

Natural Resources Systems: Programs of study related to the environment and natural resources. These may include (but are not limited to) agriculture, earth science, environmental sciences, fisheries management, forestry, horticulture, and wildlife management.

Earlier we reviewed Oregon's outcomes for the certificate of initial mastery. I believe it would be good to list here the outcomes established for Oregon's certificate of advanced mastery:

Use the context of occupational categories and life roles to advance previously learned knowledge and skills: Effectively apply, transfer, and advance knowledge and skill in communication, mathematics, arts and humanities, health and fitness, and scientific concepts and principles.

Show responsible and consistent positive behaviors: Demonstrate behaviors in self management, citizenship, employability, wellness, safety, integrity, honesty, responsibility, and lifelong learning.

Respect diversity: Develop skills for interacting with people of diverse cultures and backgrounds in the work place and in personal and family life.

Use systems and structures: Understand organizational, ecological, social and cultural, economic, and technical systems and structures, including the ability to design, monitor, adjust, and evaluate them.

Participate in group decision: Work individually and in groups to generate ideas, conceptualize solutions and strategies, and implement and evaluate decisions leading to creative problem solving skills.

Use data to communicate: Acquire, organize, analyze, evaluate, maintain, and translate into information to communicate, using appropriate formats and effective media.

Use resources to accomplish goals: Locate, select, manage, and allocate resources such as time, money, materials, space, and people to accomplish personal and work goals.

Apply technology for personal and occupational needs: Select equipment and tools, apply technology to specific tasks, and maintain and troubleshoot equipment.

Support the development of others: Support the development of others by teaching, leading, serving, collaborating, and negotiating toward common goals.

SITE COMMITTEES

Oregon's bill calls for local building site committees to be established in all schools by September 1995. These building site committees will not only eliminate the effectiveness of the elected school boards, but will also alter the authority and power of the local school committees.

Notice I did not say the school boards would be eliminated, only their effectiveness. Section 33(2) states: "Educational goals means a set of goals for educational performance, as formulated by site committees and local communities, and adopted by the district school boards." Educational goals have always been the responsibility of the elected school board. The important word in this section is the word "adopted." The school board will only be able to adopt what the site committee formulates. The board becomes an adopting agency only and cannot alter the plans of the committee in any way. They may recommend, but they can only adopt.

Another area of concern is the portion of the law which deals with local school committees. Section 34(6) states: "Whenever the decisions of any plan of the building site committee conflict with a recommendation of the local school committee established under ORS 330.667 the decision of the building site committee shall prevail." Since members of the local school committee are elected by the patrons of the school district, this represents a loss of control and authority for the elected school committee.

So if the building site committee has so much power, who's on this powerful committee and how do they get there? Section 34,(3)(a), forced into the bill by the Oregon Education Association, states, "A majority of a building site committee shall be active classroom teachers." The teachers will be selected by an election of their peers, Section 34,(3), and then members of the committee shall *appoint* parents or guardians of children attending the school, and may *appoint* representatives of the community-at-large.

In view of the above facts, what kind of increased local control do parents think they have:

A) when classroom teachers comprise the majority of the building site committee and elect themselves,

B) when decisions made by the locally elected school committee can be over-ridden by the appointed building site committee, and

C) when the elected school board can only adopt the recommendations made by the building site committee?

It is clear that our form of government is being violated. The individuals elected by the people to serve on a local school committee or on their local school board, have their authority subjugated to a body consisting of a majority of classroom teachers.

INTEGRATION OF SOCIAL SERVICES

Since it is not the task of schools to be dealing with every area of a child's life, the attempt to integrate social services onto the school site is a grave concern. Some, of course, believe the opposite; but the failures experienced by other countries should point us away from this endeavor. It is inappropriate for children to walk into their school and find a complete array of social service offices serving up food stamps, welfare assistance, health services, and child care on the way to the classroom.

Section 4a(1) of the bill states, "Services for young children and their families should be located as close to the child and the family's community as possible, encouraging community support and ownership of such services." Please note that the bill, in Section 4c(3), defines young children as "children zero through eight years of age"; and defines "services" in Section 4c(2) as "education and all other programs and services addressing one or more of a child's six basic needs as follows: stimulus, nutrition, health, safety, nurturance and shelter." Most parents are offended that the state presumes to determine the definition of young children and the services they require.

Page three of the Department of Education's task force report states: "We believe social services can be best delivered to children and families in an integrated fashion. To that end, schools, community agencies and families should work as full partners in the planning and delivery of services to children." This quite simply implies that parents should give up ownership of their children to the state in exchange for merely becoming a partner.

If the family is a partner with social services, then it follows that social services should have access to the child before it is born since the requirement includes age zero to eight. This intrusive view of the family sets the stage for agency and interagency acquisition of information about the family and decision-making authority over the child.

A recent incident in Oregon provides us with a perfect example of how the family's authority has been eroded by this philosophy. A teacher's assistant, upon learning a young student was pregnant, took her for abortion counseling. The young girl was removed from school without her parents' consent or knowledge and against her will was taken to a clinic where the abortion was performed. Upon returning to the school (parents still unaware of what had just happened to their daughter), the attendance records were altered to cover up the incident. The employee was fired but has appealed the decision, convinced she did nothing wrong.

FUNDING

Section 37 of Oregon's bill states, "Nothing in this Act is intended to be mandated without adequate funding support. Therefore those features of this Act which require significant additional funds shall not be implemented statewide until funding is available." As most states do, Oregon seems to suffer from one school finance crisis to another. It seems that no matter what the problem is, the answer is, "Send more money." As a member of the Oregon legislature, I became acutely aware of the delicate balance between parents and schools and education funding. Quite frankly, Oregon does not have the funds to initiate and fully implement this law. Funds are coming from grants, foundations, corporations, and from the federal government. Our state superintendent has implied she would even consider dipping into Oregon's Public Employee Retirement Fund, if necessary. That may or may not have been said tongue-in-cheek, but it demonstrates the fervor with which this reform is being implemented.

Oregon's superintendent has worked through Congress to obtain federal waivers on the accountability for federal monies provided for special education. Having received those waivers, the money can now be used to implement OBE, while the special education kids will be mainstreamed into the regular classroom. During this biennium, Oregon is spending $17 million, originally earmarked for economic development, for teacher retraining. And we still have not developed a new assessment tool, nor do we have an estimate for its development. The Kentucky legislature was asked to provide $80 million for the development of their assessment tool. If Oregon spent the same amount, we would be approaching $100 million before we even get to the classroom.

The Department of Education has said in public testimony before the House Education Committee that they have no idea how much will be required to fund this bill; but in a letter published in *The Oregonian* newspaper in June 1991, the Oregon Education Association was quoted as having estimated it would cost $2.5 billion to fully implement all aspects of Oregon's education reform package.

Despite the clause requiring funding to be in place before mandates become effective, Oregon is forging ahead with education reform.

The idea of a state law mandating such radical education reform may prove to be even more of a disastrous experiment than anticipated. I've reviewed the situation in Oregon so that parents and parent groups in other states may have some idea of what may be coming their way.

SO WHAT ARE OREGONIANS DOING ABOUT REFORM?

Parents, along with a good number of teachers, have launched an attempt to repeal the education reform law in Oregon. When the bill was introduced, public testimony was allowed, but most parents and educators were unaware of the magnitude of such sweeping reform and the impact it would have. When the 1993 legislature refused to review the progress of implementation, as Section 1(2) of the bill required, the momentum grew for an initiative to repeal the entire Act.

Section 1(2) states, "This Act shall be subject to review by the Sixty-seventh Legislative Assembly and each Legislative Assembly thereafter until the year 2001 for purposes of evaluating progress toward achieving the various mandates of this Act and also effecting any necessary changes."

Project Second Look was created in November 1993 as a citizens group and political action committee with the sole purpose of "taking a second look" and repealing Oregon's Education Reform Act. The initiative states:

Be it Enacted by the People of the State of Oregon: Section 1: It is the intent of this Act to repeal the Oregon Educational Act for the 21st Century. It is the directive of this Act that the 1995 Legislative Assembly shall design an elementary and secondary educational system that emphasizes academic excellence and is based on effective school practices.

The name of the group changed to Practical Reform of Education (PRE). For the next several months PRE members and other backers of the measure crisscrossed the state speaking in small and large communities. The response was incredible; when presented with the facts, parents and teachers were outraged that they were not given a proper opportunity for input before such a radical experiment was foisted upon their children. Oregonians pledged support and money for the monumental task of gathering the nearly 67,000 signatures required to place the initiative on the November ballot. Even though the grassroots effort gained incredible momentum, the initiative wording faced a lengthy and time-consuming legal challenge by a personal friend of Oregon's superintendent of public instruction.

On May 13, 1994, the initiative wording was released by the Oregon Supreme Court without any changes. The challenge was frivolous but effective. This legal maneuver was meant to delay signature gathering and discourage the backers of the measure.

By June 1, thousands of petitions were mailed across the state, giving volunteers only forty days to collect the required number of signatures. By July 8, deadline day, the effort to gather the necessary 67,000 signatures fell short by a few thousand. Volunteers, who gathered more than a thousand signatures a day, should be commended for such a valiant effort. However, the effort is not lost because of a missed deadline. The battle rages on, and the commitment to change Oregon's education reform continues.

1. See appendix one.
2. An unsuccessful attempt was made to verify all enrollment numbers with the school district.
3. CIM task force report, January 1993, 12-13.

How to Identify OBE in Your School

B y now you may be wondering how you can know if the school your children attend uses OBE. Start by developing a relationship with your children's teachers. Interview them to see if they are aware of the practices of OBE. Perhaps your choice may be to place your children in private school or to home school, but recognize this as a temporary solution. Most state bills are being designed to include *all* students, revealing the intent of the change agents behind them. For a strategy of how you can stand against OBE read chapter twelve.

To help you recognize OBE in your school, the Michigan Alliance of Families has researched and prepared a check list of practices generally common to OBE. Remember there are four stages to the implementation of OBE. Your school may only use one or a few of these practices now. The list only represents what is generally found in a system in the process of implementing OBE. It is included here for your information.

THE ABC'S OF OBE

DOES YOUR SCHOOL HAVE OBE?
IT DOES IF:

A. You have a mission or belief statement which includes "All children can learn."

B. You have a three- to five-year improvement plan.

C. An annual report is issued at district and building level.

D. You have site-based management. Have your teachers and parents been "empowered" by serving on hand-picked committees to develop a mission statement or a three- to five-year improvement plan?

E. You have cooperative learning or peer tutoring.

F. You have multi-age level grouping, having eliminated grades K-3 to start with.

G. You have replaced letter grades A-B-C-D-E-F (Bell Curve) with A-B-I (incomplete), J Curve, or no letter grading system.

H. You have replaced Carnegie Units (specified course requirements for graduation) with outcomes that must be achieved or demonstrated.

I. You have inclusive education (mainstreaming of special education and juvenile delinquents into regular classrooms).

J. You have an extended school day, year (two hundred days or more) to year-round school.

K. You have thematic teaching (all classes teach to the same theme over a certain length of time).

L. You have team teaching.

M. You have removed competition by cooperative learn-ing and group grades, as well as by the elimination of valedictorian or salutatorian.

N. You have eliminated rote memorization of facts and knowledge (content) and replaced it with what is called realistic and relevant teaching.

O. Your teachers are referred to as facilitators, coaches, or interactive participants.

P. Your teaching staff is continually involved in professional development to train them in consensus building and collaboration.

Q. You frequently hear references to Spady, Hornbeck, Sizer, Goodlad, etc.

R. You have been accredited by the North Central Association or another accreditation program, or are in the process of being accredited. Both systems are outcomes accreditation models (schools are required to target their evaluation efforts by measuring changes in students behaviors). "It is now the rule that the government must supervise accreditation. It cannot be just a private enterprise" (Dr. Ralph W. Tyler, "The History of School Evaluation In America," Create Newsletter, February 1992).

S. You have individualized education plans (IEP's) or child-centered education.

T. You have continual assessment of growth and development.

U. You have collaboration and consensus as a goal of all committees.

V. You have portfolios.

W. You stress higher order thinking skills (HOTS) or critical thinking (focuses on deciding what to believe or do) and the use of Bloom's Taxonomy (used to inculcate a prescribed set of values).

X. You have partnerships between parents and the school, the community and the school, businesses and the school, and have established foundations to help the school be more innovative.

Y. You have a school nurse, school counselor, school psychologist, school social worker, or the student assistance program, linking the schools with all community service agencies with the goal of becoming a "one stop service provider."

Z. You hear reference to mastery learning, performance-based education, Glasser's reality therapy, management by objectives (MBO), planning programming budgeting systems (PPBS), total quality management (TQM), accelerated schools, effective schools, comer schools, Johnson City Schools, Schools for the 21st Century, Sizer's coalition of essential schools, professional development schools, outcomes-driven developmental model (ODDM), all of which are outcome-based education.

Prepared and researched by:

Michigan Alliance of Families
P.O. Box 241
Flushing, MI 48433

CHAPTER TWELVE

What You Can Do

1. GET EDUCATED—GET THE FACTS

Knowledge is absolutely indispensable. An old adage says, "People are destroyed for the lack of knowledge." There are sources of good information available (see appendix four).

Develop your basic philosophy of education (i.e. values, purpose, content, and goals). Be able to articulate your position. You shouldn't merely be fighting against something. You should also be fighting *for* something. Fight for the children's future. Fight for an academically rigorous, phonics-intensive education that focuses on the national ideals that have made the United States of America the truly great country that it is.

Learn the opposing philosophy so you can recognize it when you read it, hear it, or see it. Get a copy of the law (education bill) that pertains to your state (call your state legislator). Read it and re-read it so that when people talk about the law you understand their position.[1]

2.   WRITE YOUR ELECTED OFFICIALS

We can all write to our local and state representatives. If you can write, write. If you can talk, talk. If you can support, support. Get to know your elected representatives.

Reprinted in appendix three, is a copy of legislation that passed into law in Utah. This law will protect students and families from the intrusive psychological testing going on around the country. This law strikes right at the heart of outcome-based education. A law like this in every state would send education reform back to the drawing table nationwide. All you have to do is photocopy this appendix and get it into the hands of your representative!

The person who will stop legislation in your state legislature is the individual representative or senator. You *must* communicate with your legislators. There are organizations that will help alert you of pending legislation, but no one can contact your state senator or representative for you.

3.   RUN FOR OFFICE

With all you've learned, you are ready. Run for office! That's right—school board, city council, state legislature.

These are critical times. We must realize that we cannot change the philosophy of many who have embraced this system of reform. They have taken their ideas and beliefs to the legislatures of the land to make into law. That is where we must meet them—to overcome their ideas with our ideas, to institute and re-institute the laws our founders knew would build a great nation and provide freedom for the individual.

4.   NEVER, NEVER QUIT.

Even if one bill is defeated expect another. The change agents are committed to their agenda. One small defeat won't dissuade them from their goals. They must be opposed continually. Remember the words of Thomas Jefferson, "The price of liberty is eternal vigilance." Will you be vigilant? Will you stand up and be counted on to defend the minds of today's children as they are in the process of becoming tomorrow's leaders? American education and the children's educational future rest in your hands a little while longer.

1. For a listing of resources that can help you learn more about and fight against OBE, refer to appendix four.

Oregon's OBE Law, H.B. 3565

Oregon's OBE bill is recorded here to reveal its contents and the pervasive control that the bill gives whoever happens to be in power. Critical sections are italicized to draw attention to particularly problematic and, in some cases, dangerous legislation.

HOUSE BILL 3565

Relating to education; creating new provisions; amending ORS 327.006, 327.103, 336.705, 336.730, 336.745, 339.115 and 343.415; and declaring an emergency.

Be It Enacted by the People of the State of Oregon:

SECTION 1. (1) This Act shall be known as the Oregon Educational Act for the 21st Century.

(2) The Department of Education shall be the coordinating agency for furthering implementation of this Act. *This Act shall be subject to review by the Sixty-seventh Legislative Assembly and each Legislative Assembly thereafter*

until the year 2001 for purposes of evaluating progress toward achieving the various mandate of this Act and also effecting any necessary changes.

SECTION 1a. (1) During the 1991-1992 interim, the appropriate legislative interim committee shall;

(a) Develop the form and content expected of the ongoing review described in section 1 of this Act;

(b) Notify the appropriate agencies of expectations; and

(c) Receive and evaluate regular reports from the Department of Education and other public agencies.

(2) This review outline may be changed as needed in succeeding years.

SECTION 1b. The Legislative Assembly believes that education is a major civilizing influence on the development of a humane, responsible and informed citizenry, able to adjust to and grow in a rapidly changing world. Students must be encouraged to learn of their heritage and their place in the global society. The Legislative Assembly concludes that these goals are not inconsistent with the goals to be implemented under this Act.

SECTION 2. The Legislative Assembly declares that:

(1) The State of Oregon believes that all students can learn when offered appropriate learning opportunities, *held to rigorous intellectual standards and expected to succeed.*

(2) Access to a quality education must be provided for all of Oregon's youth regardless of linguistic background, culture, race, gender, capability or geographic location.

(3) A restructured educational system is necessary to achieve the state's goals of the best educated citizens in the nation by the year 2000 and a work force equal to any in the world by the year 2010.

(4) Education programs and strategies that can substantiate a claim to the prevention of human and social costs are of highest priority to the state.

(5) The specific objectives of the Act and ORS 344.305 and 344.355 are:

(a) To achieve educational standards of performance and *outcomes* that match the highest of any in the world for all students;

(b) To establish the Certificates of Initial Mastery and Advanced Mastery as new high performance standards for all students;

(c) To establish alternative learning environments and services which offer opportunities for those experiencing difficulties in achieving the knowledge and skills necessary to obtain the Certificate of Initial Mastery;

(d) To establish early childhood programs and academic professional technical programs as part of a comprehensive educational system; and

(e) To establish partnerships among business, labor and the educational community in the development of standards for academic professional technical endorsements and provide on-the-job training and apprenticeships necessary to achieve those standards.

SECTION 3. It is the intent of the Legislative Assembly to maintain a system of public elementary and secondary schools that has the following characteristics:

(1) Provides equal and open access and educational opportunities for *all students in the state* regardless of their linguistic background, culture, race, gender, capability or geographic location;

(2) Assumes that *all students can learn* and establishes high, specific skill and knowledge expectations appropriate to the students' assessed learning rates at all instructional levels;

(3) Provides special education, compensatory education, linguistically and culturally appropriate education and other specialized programs to all students who need those services;

(4) Provides students with a solid foundation in the skills of reading, writing, problem solving, listening, speaking, critical thinking and communication, across the disciplines;

(5) Provides opportunities for students to exhibit the capacity to learn, think, reason, retrieve information and work effectively alone and in groups;

(6) Provides for a high degree of mastery in mathematics and science;

(7) Provides students with a background in social studies, foreign languages and the humanities to the end that they will function successfully and tolerantly in a *participatory democracy* and a multicultural nation and world;

(8) Provides students with a background in the visual, performing and literary arts as unique forms of communication, expression and cultural knowledge;

(9) Provides students with the knowledge and skills that will provide the opportunities to succeed in the world of work, as members of families and as citizens of a *participatory democracy*;

(10) Provides students with the knowledge and skills to take responsibility for their decisions and to make appropriate choices;

(11) Provides opportunities for students to learn through a variety of teaching strategies that focus on an individual student's learning profile including but not limited to

assessed strengths, weaknesses, learning style and interests, with appropriate intervention services;

(12) Organizes instructional groupings as heterogeneously as possible to promote the attitudes and skills necessary for democratic citizenship; and

(13) Emphasizes involvement of parents and the community in the total education of students.

SECTION 4. The Legislative Assembly recognizes that students in public elementary and secondary schools can only reach the levels of performance expected under the provisions of this Act with parental participation in the education process. It is, therefore, the policy of this state to:

(1) Require school districts to provide opportunities for parents or guardians to be involved in establishing and implementing educational goals and to participate in decision-making at the school site;

(2) Expect employers to recognize the need for parents or guardians and members of the community to participate in the education process not only for their own children but for the educational system; and

(3) Encourage employers to extend appropriate leave to parents or guardians to allow greater participation in that process during school hours.

SECTION 4a. To insure that all educational and other services for young children and their families afford the maximum opportunity possible for the personal success of the child and family members, it is the policy of this state that the following principles for serving children should be observed to the maximum extent possible in all of its educational and other programs serving young children and their families;

(1) *Services for young children and their families should be located as close to the child and the family's community as possible, encouraging community support and ownership of such services;*

(2) Services for young children and their families should reflect the importance of integration and diversity to the maximum extent possible in regard to characteristics such as race, economics, sex, creed, capability and cultural differences;

(3) Services should be designed to support and strengthen the family and be planned in consideration of existing family values, with the primary concern being the welfare of the child;

(4) Services should be designed to assure continuity of care among care givers in a given day and among service plans from year to year;

(5) Service systems should be comprehensive in nature with the flexibility to identify and address the most urgent needs in a timely manner including health, intervention and support services; and

(6) Service providers and sources of support should be coordinated and collaborative, to reflect the knowledge that no single system can serve all of the needs of the child and family.

SECTION 4b. (1) Education and other programs providing services to children and families, as identified in ORS 417.315 (4), shall:

(a) Evaluate the effectiveness of the program as related to the principles stated in ORS 417.305 and section 3 of this

Act in the earliest stages of the budget process;

(b) Articulate ways in which the program is an effective component of agency and state priorities, goals and strategies, such as those developed by the Oregon Progress Board, or to relevant research and professional standards;

(c) Establish plans, interagency partnerships, implementation practices and interactions with local and private sectors required by ORS 417.305 (3);

(d) Utilize the information generated by applicable state advisory groups and by the local planning process administered by the Oregon Community Children and Youth Services Commission in the program assessment of needs and decisions as to service delivery in a given community; and

(e) Identify barriers to improving program capability to serve the needs of young children and related recommendations, if any.

(2) The processes listed in subsection (1) of this section are for the purpose of generating interagency coordination described in ORS 417.305 so as to serve to the greatest extent possible young children and their families in a comprehensive and developmentally appropriate fashion. The information generated by these processes shall be considered as a contribution to subsequent budget decisions by state and local agencies, the Executive Department and Legislative Assembly, and as a contribution to the planning and coordination tasks of the Oregon Coordinating Council for Children and Families.

SECTION 4c. As used in sections 4a and 4b of this Act:
(1) *"Families" means a group of individuals related by*

blood, marriage or adoption, or individuals whose functional relationships are similar to those found in such associations. The family's purpose is the security, support, nurturance, love, transmission of values and facilitation of each member's growth and development, and is the primary social unit affecting a child's well-being.

(2) "Services" means education and all other programs and services addressing one or more of a child's six basic needs as follows: stimulus, nutrition, health, safety, nurturance and shelter.

(3) *"Young children" means children zero through eight years of age.*

SECTION 5. In order to achieve the goals contained in sections 2 to 4 of this Act, the State Board of Education regularly and periodically shall review and revise its common curriculum goals, including essential learning skills. The common curriculum goals shall reflect the knowledge and skill *outcomes* necessary for achieving a certificate of Initial Mastery and a Certificate of Advanced Mastery pursuant to section 2 of this Act. The review shall involve teachers and other educators, parents of students and other citizens and shall provide ample opportunity for public comment.

SECTION 6. The first review and adoption of amendments required by section 5 of this ACT shall be completed by July 1, 1992.

SECTION 7. (1) To facilitate the attainment and successful implementation of educational standards under ORS 326.051 (1)(a) and sections 2 and 3 of this Act, the State Board of Education or its designee shall assess the effectiveness of each public school district in an on-site visit no less than once every six years. Beginning in 1996, the on-site visits shall occur no less than once every three years.

(2) The board shall establish the standards, including standards of accessibility to educational opportunities, upon which the assessment is based.

(3) On a periodic basis, the board shall review existing standards and, after public hearings and consultation with local school officials, shall adopt by rule a revised set of standards.

SECTION 8. The board shall require school districts and schools to conduct self-evaluations on a biennial basis. The self-evaluation process shall involve the public in the setting of local goals. The school districts shall insure that representatives from the demographic groups of their school population are involved in the development of local improvement plans to achieve the goals. At the request of the school district, Department of Education staff shall provide ongoing technical assistance in the development and implementation of the local improvement plan. Staff members may be accompanied on their visits by distinguished Oregon educators. Local goals and improvement plans shall be made available to the public. The self-evaluations shall serve as a core component in the successful implementation of standards and shall include a review of demographics, student performance, student access to and utilization of educational opportunities and staff characteristics. However, failure to complete the self-evaluation process shall not constitute grounds for withholding of state moneys.

SECTION 9. (1) To assist school districts and schools in performing the duties described in sections 7 and 8 of this

Act, the State Board of Education shall establish a comprehensive statewide school district and *school information system to monitor outcomes,* procedures and resources of public education. This system shall provide a measure of the achievement of students in the knowledge and skill areas specified in the common curriculum goals adopted by the board.

(2) The Superintendent of Public Instruction shall collect data and produce annual school district and school profiles containing information on demographics, student performance in schools, student access to educational opportunities and staff characteristics described in this Act. In addition, school district profiles shall include a concise budget report of the school district, including revenue and expenditures of the district.

(3) The Superintendent of Public Instruction shall notify the public and the media by September 30 of each year as to the availability of school district and school profiles at school district and department offices. The superintendent shall also include notice that copies of school district and school self-evaluations can be obtained from the school districts.

SECTION 10. (1) By September 30, 1992, and by each September 30 thereafter, the Superintendent of Public Instruction shall issue an Oregon Report Card on the state of the public schools and progress toward achieving the goals contained in sections 2 and 3 of this Act.

(2) The purpose of the annual report on the state of the public schools is to monitor trends among school districts and Oregon's progress toward achieving the goals stated in this Act. The report on the state of the public schools shall be designed to:

(a) Allow educators to determine the success of their own school programs;

(b) Allow educators to sustain support for reforms demonstrated to be successful;

(c) Recognize schools for their progress and achievements; and

(d) Facilitate the use of educational resources and innovation in the most effective manner.

(3) The report shall contain, but need not be limited to:

(a) Demographic information on public school children in this state.

(b) Information pertaining to student achievement, including statewide assessment data, graduation rates and dropout rates, including progress toward achieving the education benchmarks established by the Oregon Progress Board, with arrangements by minority groupings where applicable.

(c) Information pertaining to student access to and utilization of educational and support services, including regular education programs, special education, compensatory education, bilingual and English as a second language programs, advanced course work, professional technical training, counseling services, library and media services, and transportation and food services.

(d) Information pertaining to the characteristics of the school and school staff, including assignment of teachers, experience of staff and the proportion of minorities and women represented on the teaching and administrative staff.

(e) Budget information, including source and disposition of school district operating funds and salary data.

(f) Available information gathered on a sampling basis,

in cooperation with the Occupational Program Planning System of the Employment Division, to monitor high school students in areas such as further education and training and labor market participation.

(g) Examples of exemplary programs, promising practices or other innovations in education developing in this state.

(h) Such other information as the superintendent obtains under section 9 of this Act.

(4) In the second and subsequent years that the report is issued, the report shall include a comparison between the current and previous data and an analysis of trends in public education.

SECTION 11. Sections 12 to 14 of this Act are added to and made a part of ORS 336.530 to 336.570.

SECTION 12. (1) In addition to the application described in ORS 336.555 for the 21st Century Schools Program or ORS 336.720 for the School Improvement and Professional Development program, a school district may submit proposals to:

(a) Modify laws, rules or policies;

(b) Establish nongraded school programs for students;

(c) Extend the school year or teacher and student contact hours for all students in the district or for a specified group of students;

(d) Integrate health and social services at the school site to meet the comprehensive needs of children and the families in which they live;

(e) Substantially modify traditional methods of delivering and monitoring educational services, including but not limited to the elimination of the 55-minute class period and graded classrooms and the promotion of such strategies as the use of team teaching, student-to-student mentoring, bilingual tutoring programs and inclusion of special needs population;

(f) Operate a team, small group model school with a team of teachers remaining with the same students over a period of several years using a variety of teaching techniques and research-based cooperative small groups;

(g) Develop public school choice plans to give parents, students and teachers more freedom to design and choose among programs with different emphases, both among school districts and within and among schools;

(h) Restructure programs for students, including but not limited to, applied academics, youth apprenticeships and other schoolwork models that involve, as a minimum, two-year programs;

(i) Develop new programs integrating technology into the curriculum, instruction and student assessment;

(j) Increase parent involvement in decision-making at the school site; and

(k) Restructure programs for middle level students, including, but not limited to, heterogeneous groups, integrated curriculum and staffing and appropriate teaching strategies.

(2) A district that applies under this section shall submit a proposal in accordance with rules adopted by the State Board of Education, including a requirement that the district form a district site committee composed of representatives from all affected school buildings.

(3) A proposal submitted under this section shall be approved by the school district board of directors and by the

exclusive representatives of the teachers in the district.

(4) Notwithstanding ORS 336.705 to 336.785, the State Board of Education shall give preference to applications that involve one or more of the proposals described in subsection (1) of this section or other innovative models to meet the goals of this 1991 Act.

SECTION 13. (1) By 1996, in addition to other funds available for the purposes of the 21st Century Schools Program under ORS 336.530 to 336.570 and the School Improvement and Professional development program under ORS 336.705 to 336.785, an amount equal to one percent of the State School Fund shall be used for the purposes of ORS 336.530 to 336.570 and 336.705 to 336.785 before any other distribution is made. The amount shall be distributed to eligible school districts before any other distribution is made. The amount shall be distributed to eligible school districts at the same time and in the same manner as the State School Fund is distributed. The amount distributed to any eligible school district depends on the amount approved in the school district's application.

(2) Out of the amount available for distribution under this section, an amount equal to five percent thereof shall be distributed to eligible school districts that demonstrate substantial progress in student performance as a result to changes made, taking into consideration such factors as the socioeconomic characteristics of the student population. The decision to distribute funds under this subsection shall be made by the State Board of Education on advice of the 21st Century Schools Advisory Committee.

SECTION 14. By September 1992, each school district

with more than one school shall have at least one 21st Century Schools Council established pursuant to ORS 336.745. By September 1994, all school districts shall have at least one school site with a 21st Century Schools Council. Each school site shall be required to have a 21st Century Schools Council not later than September 1995.

SECTION 15. ORS 336.730 is amended to read:

336.730. (1) The State Board of Education shall appoint a 21st Century Schools Advisory Committee to propose rules for the submission and approval of grants and programs under ORS 336.705 to 336.785, 342.782 to 342.796 and 348.120 to 348.135 and sections 12, 13, and 16 of this 1991 Act.

(2)(a) The advisory committee shall include teachers who shall constitute a majority of the 15 members, and one member from each of the following groups, at least one of whom must be a member of a minority:

(A) School administrators;

(B) School board members;

(C) Education school faculty;

(D) Classified district employees;

(E) Parents of children currently in prekindergarten through grade 12 of the pubic school system; and

(F) Members of the business and labor community.

(b) The board may appoint other citizens as considered appropriate by the board.

(3) The deadline for applications submitted by districts under ORS 336.705 to 336.785, 342.782 to 342.796 and 348.120 to 348.135 shall be April 1 preceding the school year for which they are proposed. The Department of

Education shall review all applications and shall approve or reject them no later than June 1 preceding the school year for which they are proposed.

(4) Districts that qualify for 21st Century Schools grants under ORS 336.705 to 336.785, 342.782 to 342.796 and 348.120 to 348.135 shall receive up to $1,000 per year for every full-time equivalent teacher deemed eligible for this program.

(5) Subject to ORS 291.232 to 291.260, the Superintendent of Public Instruction shall distribute grants-in-aid to eligible school districts so that at least three-quarters of the allocation due to each eligible district is received no later than February 1 of each fiscal year and the remainder when all required reports are filed with the Department of Education. If underpayments or overpayments result, adjustments shall be made in the following year.

SECTION 16. The 21st Century Schools Advisory Committee shall propose for adoption by the State Board of Education criteria for selecting Distinguished Oregon Educators who possess special skills to assist in schools beginning with the 1992-1993 school year. The 21st Century Schools Advisory Committee shall nominate educators to the Department of Education, which shall select educators who meet the criteria and who are willing to serve. With the consent of the employing school district, the educator may be assigned to assist the school districts as a member of a department team for a period not to exceed two years while retaining all rights to employment, seniority and other benefits in the educator's employing school district. During the period of the assignment, the educator of the educator's employing school district shall be compensated by the Department of Education.

SECTION 17. The State Board of Education shall prepare by July 1, 1992, a proposed set of guidelines and models to assist school districts that wish to pursue programs of choice, pursuant to sections 21 and 25 of this Act. The board shall pay particular attention to identifying obstacles that impede choice in terms of laws, rules, state and local policies and practices and transportation considerations. No program of choice under this section shall permit segregation on the basis of race, gender, capability or disabling conditions.

SECTION 18. It is the policy of this state to implement, at the earliest possible time, programs for early childhood education including prenatal care, parenting education, child-parent centers and extended Oregon prekindergarten programs. By 1996, funding shall be available for 50 percent of children eligible for Oregon prekindergarten programs, and, by 1998, full funding shall be available for all eligible children. The Oregon prekindergarten program shall continue to be operated in coordination with the federal Head Start program in order to avoid duplication of services and so as to insure maximum use of resources.

SECTION 18a. (1) In consultation with the advisory committee for the Oregon prekindergarten program, the Department of Education and the Office Community College Services shall develop a long-range plan for serving eligible children and their families and shall report to each regular session of the Legislative Assembly on the funds necessary to implement the long-range plan, including but not limited to, regular programming costs, salary enhancements and program improvement grants. The department shall determine the rate of increase in funding necessary each biennium to provide service to all children eligible for the prekindergarten program by 1998.

(2) The Department of Education and the Office of Community College Services shall include in their budget requests to the Governor, beginning with the 1993-1995 biennium, funds sufficient to implement each two-year phase of the long-range plan.

(3) Each biennial report shall include, but not be limited to, estimates of the number of eligible children and families to be served, projected cost of programs and evaluation of the programs.

SECTION 18b. When the federal Head Start program provides funding for programs for eligible children at least the 1990-1991 per child level, as described in ORS 326.600 (3), eligibility for state funded prekindergarten programs shall be expanded to include programs for children whose family income exceeds the federal Head Start limits or who are in an underserved or unserved age category. After determining the increase in income limits or age level that would make children most in need of state programs eligible for them, the State Board of Education may direct expenditure of any unexpended or unobligated funds appropriated for the biennium for eligible children to be expended for the additional children considered to be most in need. In the following biennium, the state board shall include the cost of any added program for the children most in need in its biennial budget.

SECTION 19. ORS 343.415 is amended to read:

343.415. As used in ORS 343.415 to 343.435:

(1) "Approved program" means an early childhood education program approved by the Department of Education.

(2) "At-risk children" means children who may have difficulty achieving in school and who meet criteria established by the State Board of Education.

(3) "Early childhood education" means educational programs that conform to the standards adopted by the State Board of Education and that are designed for the education and training of children who are at least three years of age but have not passed their ninth birthday, and includes all special educational programs established and operated under this chapter.

(4) "Early Childhood Improvement Program" means those programs meeting the criteria included in section 19a of this 1991 Act and complying with rules adopted by the State Board of Education.

(5) "Extended day services" means programs that serve young children and operate during hours beyond regular school time.

SECTION 19a. (1) The Department of Education shall administer the Early Childhood Improvement Program to assist public school districts in providing programs designed to improve educational services for children enrolled in grades kindergarten through three. Programs shall be based on research and proven successful practices in programs such as Head Start. The department shall evaluate the programs which receive grants under this Act and report the results of the evaluation to the Legislative Assembly.

(2) The programs shall include the following planned components:

(a) Targeted services for "at-risk" children and families, which may include but are not limited to remedial and alternative academic programs, child care, parent participation and child development services.

(b) Efforts to improve the kindergarten through third grade curriculum and educational practices so that they:

(A) Are consistent with research findings on how children learn;

(B) Are sensitive to individual differences such as cultural background and learning styles; and

(C) Encourage parent participation. Such efforts may include, but are not limited to, adapting curricula and training administrators and other staff in early childhood education and child development.

(c) Comprehensive education, health care and social services for children to be provided through interagency agreements among school districts, health care and social service providers.

(d) Evaluation of programs by goals set by the district for the program.

(e) Planned transition from prekindergarten programs to grades kindergarten through three.

(3) In addition to the components listed in subsection (4) of this section, Early Childhood Improvement Programs may include, but are not limited to, the following components:

(a) Extended day services for school age children who need care or enrichment opportunities; and

(b) Programs designed to improve the adult to child ratios in grades kindergarten to three.

(4) Plans developed by site committees at the school

building level as described in ORS 336.745; and

(a) Demonstrated consistency with the local assessments and plans resulting from the juvenile program planning described in ORS 417.415.

(5) Public school districts or consortia of such districts with education service districts are eligible to receive funds under this Act. Funds shall be available to districts with approved applications on a per child basis for the district's children enrolled in kindergarten through grade three. Funds not allocated shall be prorated to the districts with approved applications not later than the end of the fiscal year for which the allocation is made.

(6) If the district plan proposes use of innovative instructional materials, the State Board of Education, pursuant to ORS 337.050, may waive the use of such instructional materials as might otherwise have been required.

SECTION 19b. The Superintendent of Public Instruction shall appoint an advisory committee composed of public school teachers, district school board members, administrators, social service and health professionals, parents, early childhood specialists and business and community members to assist with the establishment of the rules and program requirements under ORS 343.415 and sections 19a to 19e of this Act. The advisory committee shall be disbanded on June 30, 1992.

SECTION 19c. (1) The State Board of Education shall adopt rules for the establishment of the Early Childhood Improvement Program. Rules shall require school districts to include in their applications cooperative efforts with other programs for young children.

(2) The Department of Education shall review and approve applications by July 1 of each year.

SECTION 19d. Application approval shall commence on January 1, 1992, to be approved not later than July 1, 1992.

SECTION 19e. The initial rules to implement sections 19a to 19e of this Act shall be adopted not later than December 31, 1991.

SECTION 19f. (1) By the 1992 school year, the Department of Education shall recommend models for use by school districts for developmentally appropriate nongraded primary programs for children enrolled in prekindergarten through the primary grades. The models shall be done in consultation with:

(a) *Teachers, parents, administrators and classified school employees from schools and Oregon prekindergarten programs that currently provide:*

(A) *Developmentally appropriate nongraded primary programs;*

(B) Comprehensive health and social services;

(C) Active parent involvement;

(D) Extended day services; or

(E) Staff development programs in developmentally appropriate practices;

(b) Higher education faculty representatives from the fields of education, human development and family services; and

(c) Community college representatives from the field of early childhood education.

(2) The State Board of Education shall report to the 1993 regular session of the Legislative Assembly on the feasibility of all school districts implementing nongraded primary programs, including strategies for prevention of failure and early intervention for students requiring special assistance.

(3) Plans for early childhood education shall include a recommended funding formula and implementation process that recognize the need for flexible models to meet local needs and shall include strategies that:

(a) Reduce the ratio of students to teachers and other trained adults in the classroom;

(b) Utilize trained classified and other support personnel;

(c) Coordinate comprehensive health and social services to parents and families;

(d) Provide for extended day services to children either through coordination with existing community provider or through school-sponsored programs;

(e) Improve the curriculum and instructional practices consistent with research;

(f) Provide materials, supplies and equipment needed to carry out developmentally appropriate programs;

(g) Provide in-service training in developmentally appropriate practices for staff;

(h) Encourage parent or guardian participation and education regarding developmentally appropriate practices for young children;

(i) Recognize the necessity for appropriate physical facilities to carry out this subsection;

(j) Encourage heterogeneous groupings of students and discourage negative labeling of children's learning levels; and

(k) Develop nongraded primary models that are culturally and linguistically appropriate.

SECTION 19g. The Department of Education shall study and develop plans to insure that the school restructuring efforts framed in this Act address the unique learning and developmental needs of the middle educational levels between the early childhood education and Certificate of Initial Mastery levels detailed in this Act. This shall be done in consultation with teachers, parents and administrators from schools serving middle level students. The Department of Education shall report to the Sixty-seventh Legislative Assembly as to agency plans and legislative considerations needed on the matter.

SECTION 20. (1) By the end of the 1996-1997 school year, every student shall have the opportunity by 16 years of age or upon completing grade 10 to obtain a Certificate of Initial Mastery.

(2) The State Board of Education shall prescribe the standards, pursuant to sections 2 and 3 of this Act, that a student must meet in order to obtain a Certificate of Initial Mastery. The Certificate of Initial Mastery shall be based on a series of *performance-based assessments benchmarked to mastery levels at approximately grades 3, 5, 8 and 10 including, but not limited to, work samples, tests and portfolios.* Students shall be allowed to collect credentials over a period of years, culminating in a project or exhibition that demonstrates attainment of the required knowledge and skills.

(3) Requirements for the Certificate of Initial Mastery shall:

(a) Assure that a student has the knowledge and skills to read, write, problem solve, think critically and communicate across the disciplines, at national levels by the year 2000 and at international levels by the year 2010; and

(b) Assure that students exhibit the capacity to learn, think, reason, retrieve information and work effectively alone and in groups.

(4) A Certificate of Initial Mastery shall be required for entry into college preparatory and academic professional technical programs leading to the appropriate endorsement.

(5) On or before January 1, 1995, each school district shall present a plan to the Department of Education setting forth the steps the district has taken to insure that its curriculum meets the requirements necessary for the students of the district to obtain Certificates of Initial Mastery. Each district's plan shall include options for achieving the certificate through alternative educational programs, including, but not limited to, those offered at Learning Centers established pursuant to section 24 of this Act.

(6) The provisions of this section may be applied individually as appropriate to students enrolled in special education programs under ORS chapter 343.

(7) The Department of Education shall develop procedures to accommodate out-of-state students, students taught by a parent or private teachers pursuant to ORS 339.035, private school students transferring into pubic schools and migrant children from other states and countries.

SECTION 21. (1) The Department of Education shall implement an assessment system for all students, including performance-based assessment of the knowledge and skills necessary to achieve the standards for each mastery level leading to the Certificate of Initial Mastery. However, until this plan is operational, assessment shall continue at grades 3, 5, 8 and 10.

(2) The State Board of Education by rule shall establish criteria for determining whether students have demonstrated the knowledge and skills necessary to perform successfully at each level in the manner described in section 20 of this Act, beginning with the 1994/1995 school year.

(3) The resident district shall be accountable for the student's satisfactory progress, as set forth in subsection (4) of this section, or be responsible for finding alternative learning environments, with the concurrence of the student's parents or guardian.

(4) *If, at any point, a student is not making satisfactory progress toward attainment of the standard at grades 3, 5, 8, and 10, including the Certificates of Initial Mastery and Advanced Mastery, the school district shall make additional services available to the student, that may include but need not be limited to:*

(a) A restructured school day;

(b) Additional school days;

(c) Individualized instruction and other alternative instructional practices; and

(d) *Family evaluation and social services, as appropriate.*

(5) If the student to whom additional services have been made available fails to demonstrate the knowledge and skills required at the mastery level within one year after the determination under subsection (2) of this section, even though the student would be or is promoted to the next level, the student shall be allowed to transfer to another public school in the district or to a public school in another district that agrees to accept the student. The district that receives the student shall be entitled to payment. The payment shall consist of:

(a) An amount equal to the district expenses from its local revenues for each student in average daily membership, payable by the resident district in the same year; and

(b) Any state and federal funds the attending district is entitled to receive payable as provided on ORS 332.595 (2).

SECTION 22. (1) It is the policy of the State of Oregon to encourage students to remain in school and to earn their Certificates of Initial Mastery and Certificates of Advanced Mastery before seeking employment during the regular school year.

(2) With the advice of the Wage and Hour Commission and in consultation with the Workforce Quality Council and the State Board of Higher Education, the State Board of Education shall propose rules applicable to the continuation of education of minors who have not obtained the Certificate of Initial Mastery and the Certificate of Advanced Mastery *and who seek to be employed during the regular school year. The proposed rules shall provide opportunities to partici-pate in the employment decision-making relating to the minor, by the minor, the minor's parents or guardian, local school authorities and the potential employer.*

(3) The state board shall submit its proposed rules to the Legislative Assembly for review not later than January 1, 1993.

(4) If the state board's proposed rules are approved by the Legislative Assembly, the state board's proposed rules shall take effect July 1, 1997.

(5) Nothing in this section is intended to affect the authority of the Wage and Hour Commission to regulate the employment conditions of minors under ORS 653.305 to 653.545.

SECTION 23. (1) The Oregon Workforce Quality Council, established under section ____, chapter ____, Oregon Laws 1991 (Enrolled House Bill 3133), in consultation with the Department of Education, the Office of Community College Services, the Bureau of Labor and Industries, the Economic development Department and the Department of Human Resources, shall propose policies and strategies consistent with this Act.

(2) The Oregon Workforce Quality Council's policies and strategies must take into account that:

(a) The state must promote innovative thinking with respect to the curriculum and educational delivery system of Oregon public schools;

(b) The state must require of all youth a level of achievement that prepares them to pursue college, professional technical programs, apprenticeships, work-based training and school-to-work programs;

(c) Greater employer investment is essential in the ongoing training of all workers to meet work force needs;

(d) The state must encourage Oregon businesses to improve productivity by creating high performance work organizations that provide high skills and high wage opportunities for youth and adults; and

(e) All employment-related training, education and job placement services and sources of funds must be coordinated among state agencies and boards and must complement the state's overall efforts on behalf of youth adults.

SECTION 24. (1) By January 1, 1995, the Department of Education in consultation with the Office of Community College Services and the Oregon Workforce Quality Council shall formulate an implementation plan for approval by the State Board of Education establishing learning environments that may include Learning Centers designed to assist students who have left school in obtaining the Certificate of Initial Mastery through the use of teaching strategies, technology and curricula that emphasize the latest research and best practice.

(2) The Learning Centers shall also provide the integration of existing local and community programs that provide any part of the services needed to assist individuals in obtaining the Certificate of Initial Mastery.

(3) The plan for the centers shall promote means of identifying, coordinating and integrating existing resources and may include:

(a) Day care services;

(b) After-school child care;

(c) Parental training;

(d) Parent and child education;

(e) English as a second language or bilingual services for limited proficiency students;

(f) Health services or referral to health services;

(g) Housing assistance;

(h) Employment counseling, training and placement;

(i) Summer and part-time job development;

(j) Drug and alcohol abuse counseling; and

(k) Family crisis and mental health counseling.

(4) Education service districts, school districts or schools, or any combination thereof, shall contact any eligible elementary or secondary school student and the student's family if the student has ceased to attend school to encourage the student's enrollment at a Learning Center. If the student of

the family cannot be located, the name and last known address shall be reported to the Learning Center or school nearest the address. The Learning Center shall attempt to determine of that student or family is being provided services by this state and shall seek to assist the student or family in any appropriate manner.

(5) The Department of Education shall monitor the Learning Centers and periodically report their progress to the State Board of Education and the Oregon Workforce Quality Council. The department may recommend integration of existing services if it determines that such services can be provided more effectively at the centers.

(6) The Learning Centers shall be entitled to payment by the district in which the student resides until the student reaches 21 years of age or has earned the Certificate of Initial Mastery, whichever occurs earlier, pursuant to the rules established by the State Board of Education. The payment shall be in an amount not to exceed the cost of the student's participation in the program. A school district shall not receive state funds for the student in an amount that exceeds the cost of the student's participation in the program. The payment shall consist of:

(a) An amount equal to the district expenses from its local revenues for each student in average daily membership, payable by the resident district in the same year;

(b) Any state and federal funds that the district is entitled to receive; and

(c) Any supplemental funds available to the resident district necessary to provide appropriate education services to the student consistent with any previous services provided by the resident district.

(7) Adults who wish to pursue a Certificate of Initial Mastery may attend a Learning Center and pay tuition for services.

(8)Learning centers may establish advisory committees involving representatives from the site committees in those districts, and including a majority of teachers.

SECTION 25. (1) Beginning with the 1997-1998 school year, any student who has received a Certificate of Initial Mastery shall be entitled to attend any public educational institution that enrolls the student and provides a program leading to the achievement of a Certificate of Advanced Mastery and a college preparatory or academic professional technical indorsement, or both, and meets the requirements of the State Board of Education.

(2) In establishing the requirements for Certificates of Advanced Mastery with endorsements, the State Board of Education shall facilitate the movement between the endorsements and shall encourage choice and mobility so as to enhance a student's opportunities to maximize exposure to the full range of educational experiences.

(3) The institution shall be reimbursed for the student's tuition by the district in which the student resided pursuant to ORS 339.115 and rules of the State Board of Education, in an amount not to exceed the student's tuition or the amount the district receives for the student from state funds, whichever is less. A school district shall not receive state funds for the student in an amount that exceeds the student's tuition. Any adult who wishes to pursue an indorsement, or any student having earned the Certificate of Advanced Mastery or who has attained 19 years of age and who wishes

to continue a program may do so by paying tuition. As used in this section, "public educational institution" does not include a public school to which a student has transferred under section 21 of this Act.

(4) A high school diploma issued by an accredited private or out-of-state secondary school as signifying successful completion of grade 12 shall be considered acceptable in lieu of a Certificate of Advanced Mastery for purposes of any rights or privileges that attach to the holder of a Certificate of Advanced Mastery.

SECTION 26. ORS 339.115 is amended to read:

339.115. (1) Except as provided in ORS 336.165 authorizing tuition for courses not part of the regular school program, the district school board shall admit free of charge to the schools of the district all persons between the ages of 5 and 19 residing therein. The person whose 19th birthday occurs during the school year shall continue to be eligible for a free and appropriate public education for the remainder of the school year. However, a district school board may admit other nonresident persons, determine who is not a resident of the district and may fix rates of tuition for nonresidents. A district must admit an otherwise eligible person who has not yet attained 21 years of age if the person is:

(a) Receiving special education; or

(b) Shown to be in need of additional education in order to receive a Certificate of Initial or Advanced Mastery.

(2) The person shall apply to the board of directors of the school district or residence for admission after the 19th birthday as provided in subsection (1) of this section. A person aggrieved by a decision of the local board may appeal to

the State Board of Education. The decision of the state board is final and not subject to appeal.

(3) Notwithstanding ORS 332.595 (1), a school district shall not exclude from admission a child located in the district solely because the child does not have a fixed place of residence or solely because the child is not under the supervision of a parent, guardian or person in a parental relationship.

(4) A child entering the first grade during the fall term shall be considered to be six years of age if the sixth birthday of the child occurs on or before September 1. A child entering kindergarten during the fall term shall be considered to be five years of age if the fifth birthday of the child occurs on or before September 1. However, nothing in this section prevents a district school board from admitting free of charge a child whose needs for cognitive, social and physical development would best be met in the school program, as defined by policies of the district school board, to enter school even though the child has not attained the minimum age requirement but is a resident of the district.

SECTION 27. (1) Commencing no later than September 1997, each school district shall institute programs that allow students to qualify for a Certificate of Advanced Mastery with college preparatory and academic professional technical endorsements. Study may be undertaken in a public school, community college or public professional technical school, or any combination thereof, and must involve at least two years of study or a combination of work and study. The certificate program must include a comprehensive educational component.

(2) The student must demonstrate mastery of knowledge and skills on performance-based assessments, where possible, using work samples, tests, portfolios, or other means. All courses necessary for either indorsement shall be available to students irrespective of their chosen indorsement area.

SECTION 28 (1) The Department of Education, the Office of Community College Services and the Oregon State System of Higher Education in consultation with the Oregon Workforce Quality Council shall develop comprehensive education and training programs for two-year to five-year academic professional technical endorsements and associate degrees.

(2) In addition to the requirements of subsection (1) of this section, there may be established a process for industrial certification and a sequence of advanced certification that could be obtained throughout a person's career.

(3) Work groups, including teachers, community members and representatives of business and labor, may be appointed to offer specialized information concerning knowledge and skill requirements for occupations.

(4) Not later than January 1, 1994, no fewer than six broad occupational categories shall be identified, with additional categories added in future years. The education and training curriculum and achievement standards for each occupation and trade selected for students to achieve academic professional technical endorsements or associate degrees in the occupational categories selected shall be developed and available for school districts, community colleges and other training sites.

(5) The curriculum developed for endorsements and

associate degrees must include, but need not be limited to, opportunities for structured work experiences, cooperative work and study programs, on-the-job training and apprenticeship programs in addition to other subjects.

(6) In considering where a student can most effectively and economically obtain the knowledge and skills required for the indorsement or the associate degree, the Oregon Workforce Quality Council may recommend integrating 2 + 2 Programs, the Job Training Partnership Act program, apprenticeship programs and any other state or federal job training program.

SECTION 29. A student who has obtained a Certificate of Initial Mastery and who enrolls in a college preparatory program shall be entitled to receive a Certificate of Advanced Mastery with college preparatory indorsement if the student meets the requirements established by rule of the State Board of Education, prepared in consultation with the State Board of Higher Education.

SECTION 30. By 1993, the State Board of Higher Education, in consultation with the State Board of Education, the Teacher Standards and Practices Commission and the Oregon Workforce Quality Council, shall develop programs of research, teacher and administrator preparation and continuing professional development that are responsive to the needs of the educational system and related to the goals of this Act.

SECTION 31. (1) In pursuit of excellence, it is the policy of the State of Oregon to encourage and evaluate the development of extended school year programs to meet the objectives of this Act. The Department of Education shall research the feasibility, including the potential fiscal impact to school districts, of extended school year models being used in the United States and other countries to facilitate the implementation of such programs.

(2) To achieve the goals as set forth in sections 2 to 4 of this Act, the State Board of Education shall lengthen the school year by hours equivalent to 185 days by the 1996 school year, to 200 days by the 2000 school year and to 220 days by the 2010 school year with adequate days available for staff development, home visits, parent or student conferences, or both, and other activities to insure the educational development of students, subject to review by the Legislative Assembly and subject to implementation of this Act.

SECTION 32, ORS 327.103 is amended to read:

327.103 (1) All school districts are presumed to maintain a standard school until the school has been found to be deficient by the Superintendent of Public Instruction, pursuant to standards and rules of the State Board of Education.

(2) *If any deficiencies are not corrected before the beginning of the school year next following the date of the finding of deficiency and if an extension has not been granted under subsection (3) of this section, the Superintendent of Public Instruction may withhold portions of State School Fund moneys otherwise allocated to the district for operating expenses until such deficiencies are corrected unless the withholding would create an undue hardship, as determined pursuant to rules of the State Board of Education.*

(3) Within 90 days of the finding of deficiency, a school district found not to be in compliance shall submit a plan, acceptable to the Superintendent of Public Instruction, for

meeting standardization requirements. A team of Department of Education staff, with Distinguished Oregon Educators, when feasible, operating under the direction of the Department of Education, shall visit the school district and offer technical assistance, as needed, in the preparation and implementation of the plan. When an acceptable plan for meeting standardization requirements has been submitted, the Superintendent of Public Instruction may allow an extension of time, not to exceed 12 months, if the superintendent determines that such deficiencies cannot be corrected or removed before the beginning of the next school year. However, no extension shall be granted if it is possible for a district to correct the deficiency through merger. For the period of the extension of time under this subsection, the school shall be considered a conditionally standards school.

(4) *Any district failing to submit a plan for meeting standardization requirements within the time specified shall receive no further State School Fund moneys until a plan acceptable to the Superintendent of Public Instruction is submitted irrespective of the district's being given one year in which to comply.*

SECTION 33. ORS 336.705 is amended to read:

336.705 As used in ORS 336.705 to 336.785, 343.796 and 348.120 to 348.135: (1) "Administrator" includes all persons whose duties require administrative certificates.

(2) *"Educational goals" means a set of goals for educational performance, as formulated by site committees and local communities, and adopted by district school boards,* according to provisions of ORS 336.705 to 336.785, 342.782 to 342.796 and 348.120 to 348.135, to encourage greater accountability between schools and the community, and better to assess the effectiveness of educational programs, including the profes-

sional growth and career opportunity programs, described in ORS 336.705 to 336.785, 342.782 to 342.796 and 348.120 to 348.135.

(3) "Index of teaching and learning conditions" means the system for the collection and analysis of relevant educational data by schools, districts and the state for the purpose of assessing the educational effectiveness of schools and programs.

(4) "Parents" means parents or guardians of students currently enrolled in a public school providing education in prekindergarten through grade 12.

(5) "School district" means a school district, an education service district, a state-operated school or any legally constituted combination of such entities that submits an application under ORS 336.720.

(6) "21st Century Schools Council" means a body composed of teachers, classified district employees, administrators, parents of students and others, constituted under ORS 336.745.

(7) "Teacher" means all certificated employees in the public schools or employed by an education service district who have direct responsibility for instruction, coordination of educational programs or supervision of teachers, and who are compensated for their services from public funds. "Teacher" does not include a school nurse as defined in ORS 342.455 or a person whose duties require an administrative certificate.

SECTION 34. ORS 336.745 is amended to read:

336.745 (1) To the extent practicable, the establishment of school goals, the development and use of indexes of teaching and learning conditions and the administration of grants-in-aid for the professional development of teachers and classified district employees shall be delegated to site committees that are established at the school building level.

(2) A building site committee established under ORS 336.705 to 336.782, 342.796 and 348.120 to 348.135 shall be composed of teachers, classified district employees, building administrators and parents of students. *Members of the committee shall appoint parents* or guardians of children attending the school and may appoint representatives of the community at-large.

(3) *Teachers, classified district employees, building administrators and any designated representatives of the district school board who serve on a building site committee shall be selected by the direct election of peers under the following conditions:*

(a) *A majority of a building site committee shall be active classroom teachers.*

(b) The principal of a school or the principal's designee shall be a member of a building site committee.

(4) The duties of a building site committee under ORS 336.705 to 336.785, 342.796 and 348.120 to 348.135 shall include, but are not limited to:

(a) the development and implementation of a plan to improve the professional growth and career opportunities of a school's staff;

(b) The improvement of its instructional program; and

(c) The development and coordination of the implementation of this 1991 Act at the school site.

(5) A district may establish a district site committee to assist in the administration of grants under ORS 336.705 to 336.785, 342.782 to 342.796 and 348.120 to 348.135.

Such district site committees shall be composed of teachers, classified district employees, administrators, parents of students and at least one member appointed by the school board. Teachers shall comprise one-half of such committees and shall be appointed by the certified or recognized bargaining unit, if any, for teachers in the district. Classified district employees shall be appointed by the recognized bargaining unit, if any, for classified employees in the district.

(6) *Whenever the decision of any plan of the building site committee conflicts with a recommendation of the local school committee established under ORS 330.667, the decision of the building site committee shall prevail.*

SECTION 35. ORS 327.006 is amended to read:

327.006. As used in ORS 327.006 to 327.053, 327.059, 327.063 and 327.072 to 327.133:

(1) "Aggregate days membership" means the sum of days present and absent, according to the rules of the State Board of Education, of all resident pupils when school is actually in session during a certain period. The aggregate days membership of kindergarten pupils shall be calculated on the basis of a half-day program.

(2) "Aggregate daily membership" means the aggregate days membership of a school during a certain period divided by the number of days the school was actually in session during the same period. However, if a district school board adopts a class schedule that operates throughout the year for all or any schools in the district, average daily membership shall be computed by the Department of Education so that the resulting average daily membership will not be higher or lower than if the board had not adopted such schedule.

(3) "Capital outlay" means any expenditure by a school district for materials of any sort, except replacements, which increase the value of the school plant or equipment.

(4) "Debt service" means any payment made by a school district as a result of the issuance of bonds or negotiable interest-bearing warrants authorized by the electors of the district.

(5) "Kindergarten" means a kindergarten program that conforms to the standards and rules adopted by the State Board of Education.

(6) "Net operating expenditures" means the sum of expenditures of a school district in kindergarten through grade 12 for administration, instruction, attendance and health services, operation of plant, maintenance of plant, fixed charges and tuition for resident students attending in another district, as determined in accordance with the rules of the State Board of Education, but net operating expenditures does not include transportation, food service, student body activities, community services, capital outlay, debt service or expenses incurred for nonresident students.

(7)(a) "Resident pupil" means any pupil:

(A) Whose legal school residence is within the boundaries of a school district reporting the pupil, if the district is legally responsible for the education of the pupil, except that "resident pupil" does not include a pupil who pays tuition or for whom the parent pays tuition or for whom the district does not pay tuition for placement outside the district; or

(B) Whose legal residence is not within the boundaries of the district reporting the pupil but attends school in the district with the written consent of the affected school district boards. However, such written agreements shall not apply to pupils attending high school under ORS 335.090.

(b) "Resident pupil" includes a pupil admitted to a school district under ORS 339.115 (3).

(8) "Standard school" means a school meeting the standards set by the rules of the State Board of Education.

(9) "Assessed value" means the assessed value of the property within the district, as shown upon the assessment roll as of January 1 of the calendar year in which the last preceding fiscal year of the school district commenced for which a value has been certified pursuant to ORS 311.105. However, where schools for all 13 grades are not operated or provided for by the same district, eight and one-third percent of the assessed value shall be attributed to a district for each grade.

SECTION 36. (1) The amendments to ORS 336.705 by section 33 of this Act are intended to change the name of the site committee or building site committee to the 21st Century Schools Council.

(2) For the purpose of harmonizing and clarifying statute sections published in Oregon Revised Statutes, the Legislative Counsel may substitute for words designating the site committee or building site committee from which duties, functions or powers are transferred by this Act, wherever they occur in Oregon Revised Statutes, other words designating the 21st Century Schools Council to which such duties, functions or powers are transferred.

SECTION 37. *Nothing in this Act is intended to be mandated without adequate funding support. Therefore, those features of this Act which require significant additional funds shall not be implemented statewide until funding is available.*

SECTION 38. (1) *The State Board of Education shall adopt rules, as necessary for the statewide implementation of this Act.* The rules shall be prepared in consultation with appropriate representatives from the educational and business and labor communities.

(2) Beginning in the 1991-1993 biennium, the Department of Education shall be responsible for coordinating research, planning and public discussion so that activities necessary to the implementation of this Act can be achieved. Actions by the department to fulfill this responsibility may include, but are not limited to:

(a) Updating common curriculum goals to meet international standards;

(b) Developing performance-based assessment mechanisms;

(c) Establishing criteria for Certificates of Initial Mastery and Advanced Mastery, and for benchmarks at grades 3, 5, 8 and 10;

(d) Researching and developing models for nongraded primaries;

(e) Establishing criteria for early childhood improvement programs;

(f) Amending the application process for school improvement grants;

(g) Researching and developing educational choice plans;

(h) Working with the Oregon Workforce Quality Council and the Office of Community College Services to develop no fewer than six broad occupational choices for Certificates of Advanced Mastery;

(i) Establishing criteria for the selection of Distinguished Oregon Educators;

(j) Establishing criteria for learning environments that may include alternative learning centers; and

(k) Working with the Wage and Hour Commission in consultation with the Workforce Quality Council and the State Board of Higher Education to propose rules for continuation of the education of minors seeking employment during the regular school year.

SECTION 39. As used in chapter __, Oregon Laws 1991 (Enrolled House Bill 3133) "oversee" means general overview and coordination of effort but does not include general operating or administrative responsibility.

SECTION 40. *This Act being necessary for the immediate preservation of the public peace, health and safety, an emergency is declared to exist, and this Act takes effect July 1, 1991.*

Passed by House June 4, 1991.
Repassed by House June 27, 1991.
Passed by Senate June 25, 1991.
Repassed by Senate June 27, 1991.
Received by Governor July 25, 1991.
Approved by Governor July 31, 1991.

Mastery Learning Reconsidered

This research from Johns Hopkins University demonstrates clearly the negative results of OBE.

MASTERY LEARNING RECONSIDERED
GRANT NO. OERI-G-86-0006
ROBERT E. SLAVIN
REPORT NO. 7 JANUARY 1987

Center for Research on Elementary and Middle Schools
The Johns Hopkins University
3505 North Charles Street
Baltimore, MD 21218

Published by the Center for Research on Elementary and Middle Schools, supported as a national research and development center by funds from the Office of Education Research and Improvement. US Department of Education.

Abstract

Several recent reviews and meta-analyses have claimed extraordinarily positive effects of master learning on student achievement, and Bloom (1984) has hypothesized that mastery-based treatments will soon be able to produce "two-sigma" (i.e., two standard deviation) increases in achievement. This article examines the literature on achievement effects of practical applications of group-based mastery learning in elementary and secondary schools over periods of at least four weeks, using a review technique, "best-evidence synthesis," which combines features of meta-analytic and traditional narrative reviews. The review found essentially no evidence to support the effectiveness of group-based mastery learning on standardized achievement measures. On experimenter-made measures, effects were generally positive but moderate in magnitude, with little evidence that effects maintained over time. These results are discussed in light of the coverage vs. mastery dilemma posed by group-based mastery learning.

MASTERY LEARNING RECONSIDERED

The term "mastery learning" refers to a large and diverse category of instructional methods. The principal defining characteristic of mastery learning methods is the establishment of a criterion level of performance held to represent "mastery" of a given skill or concept, frequent assessment of student progress toward the mastery criterion, and provision of corrective instruction to enable students who do not initially meet the mastery criterion to do so on later parallel assessments (see Bloom, 1976: Block & Anderson, 1975). Bloom (1976) also includes an emphasis on appropriate use of such instructional variables as cues, participation, feedback, and reinforcement as elements of mastery learning, but these are not uniquely defining characteristics; rather, what defines mastery learning approaches is the organization of time and resources to ensure that most students are able to master instructional objectives.

There are three primary forms of mastery learning. One, called the Personalized System of Instruction (PSI) or the Keller Plan (Keller, 1986), is used primarily at the post-secondary level. In this form of mastery learning, unit objectives are established for a course of study and tests are developed for each. Students may take the test (or parallel forms of it) as many times as they wish until they achieve a passing score. To do this, students typically work on self-instructional materials and/or work with peers to learn the course content, and teachers may give lectures more to supplement than to guide the learning process (see Kulik, Kulik, and Cohen, 1979). A related form of mastery learning is continuous progress (e.g., Cohen, 1977), where students work on individualized units entirely at their own rate. Continuous progress mastery learning programs differ from other individualized models only in that they establish mastery criteria for unit tests and provide corrective activities to students who do not meet these criteria the first time.

The third form of mastery learning is called group-based mastery learning, or Learning for Mastery (LFM) (Block & Anderson, 1975). This is by far the most commonly used form of mastery learning in elementary and secondary schools. In group-based mastery learning the teacher instructs the entire class at one pace. At the end of each unit of instruction a "formative test" is given, covering the unit's content. A mastery criterion, usually in the range of 80-90 percent correct, is established for this test. Any students who do not achieve the mastery criterion on the formative test receive corrective instruction, which may take the form of tutoring by the teacher or by students who did achieve at the criterion level, small group sessions in which teachers go over skills or concepts students missed, alternative activities or materials for students to complete independently, and so on. In describing this form of master learning, Block and Anderson (1975) recommend that corrective activities be different from the kinds of activities used in initial instruction. Following the corrective instruction, students take a parallel formative or "summative" test. In some cases only one cycle of formative test-corrective instruction-parallel test is used, and the class moves on even if several students still have not achieved the mastery criterion; in others, the cycle may be repeated two or more times until virtually all students have gotten a passing score. All students who achieve the mastery criterion at any point are generally given an "A" on the unit, regardless of how many tries it took for them to reach the criterion score.

The most recent full-scale review of research on mastery learning was published more than a decade ago, by Block and Burns (1976). However, in recent years two meta-analyses of research in this area have appeared, one by Kulik, Kulik, and Bangert-Drowns (1986) and one by Guskey and Gates (1985, 1986). Meta-analyses characterize the impact of a treatment on a set of related outcomes using a common metric called "effect size," the post test score for the experimental group minus that for the control group divided by the control group's standard deviation (see Glass, McGaw, and Smith, 1981). For example, an effect size of 1.0 would indicate that on the average, an experimental group exceeded a control group by one standard deviation; the average member of the experimental group would score at the level of a student in the 84th percentile of the control group's distribution.

Both of the recent meta-analyses of research on mastery learning report extraordinary positive effects of this method on student achievement. Kulik et al. (1986) find mean effect sizes of 0.52 for pre-college studies and 0.54 for college studies. Guskey and Gates (1985) claim effect sizes of 0.94 at the elementary level (grades 1-8), 0.72 at the high school level, and 0.65 at the college level. Further, Walberg (1984) reports a mean effect size of 0.81 for "science mastery learning" and Lysakowski and Walberg (1982) estimate an effect size for "cues, participation, and corrective feedback," principal components of mastery learning, at 0.97. Bloom (1984, p. 7) claims an effect size of 1.00 "when mastery learning procedures are done systematically and well," and has predicted that forms of mastery learning will be able to consistently produce achievement effects of "two sigma" (i.e., effect sizes of 2.00). To put these effect sizes in perspective, consider that the mean effect size for randomized studies of one-to-one adult tutoring reported by Glass, Cohen, Smith, and Filby (1982) was 0.62 (see Slavin, 1984). If the effects of mastery learning instruction approach or exceed those for one-to-one tutoring, then mastery learning is indeed a highly effective instructional method.

The purpose of the present article is to review the research on the effects of group-based mastery learning on the achievement of elementary and secondary students in an attempt to understand the validity and the practical implications of these findings. The review uses a method for synthesizing large literatures called "best-evidence synthesis" (Slavin, 1986), which combines the uses of effect size as a common metric of treatment effect with narrative review procedures. Before synthesizing the "best evidence" on practical applications of mastery learning, the following sections discuss the theory on which group-based mastery learning is based, how that theory is interpreted in practice, and problems inherent to research on the achievement effects of mastery learning.

MASTERY LEARNING IN THEORY AND PRACTICE

The theory on which mastery learning is based is quite compelling. Particularly in such hierarchically organized subjects as mathematics, reading and foreign language, failure to learn prerequisite skills is likely to interfere with students' learning of later skills. For example, if a student fails to learn to subtract, he or she is sure to fail in learning long division. Instruction is directed toward ensuring that nearly all students learn each skill in a hierarchical sequence, then students will have the prerequisite skills necessary to enable them to learn the later skills. Rather than accepting the idea that differences in student aptitudes will lead to corresponding differences in student achievement, mastery learning theory holds that instructional time and resources should be used to bring all students up to an acceptable level of achievement. Put another way, mastery learning theorists suggest that rather than holding instructional time constant and allowing achievement to vary (as in traditional instruction), achievement level should be held constant and time allowed to vary (see Bloom, 1968; Carroll, 1963).

In an extreme form, the central contentions of mastery

learning theory are almost tautologically true. If we establish a reasonable set of learning objectives and demand that every student achieve them at a high level regardless of how long that takes, then it is virtually certain that all students will ultimately achieve that criterion. For example, imagine that students are learning to subtract two-digit numbers with renaming. A teacher might set a mastery criterion of 80 percent on a test of two-digit subtraction. After some period of instruction, the class is given a formative test, and let's say half of the class achieves at the 80 percent level. The teacher might then work with the "non-masters" group for one or more periods, and then give a parallel test. Say that half of the remaining students pass this time (25 percent of the class). If the teacher continues this cycle indefinitely, then all or almost all students will ultimately learn the skill, although it may take a long time for this to occur. Such a procedure would also accomplish two central goals of mastery learning, particularly as explicated by Bloom (1976): To reduce the variation in student achievement and to reduce or eliminate any correlation between aptitude and achievement. Since all students must achieve at a high level on the subtraction objective but students who achieve the criterion early cannot go on to new material, there is a ceiling effect built in to the procedure which will inherently cause variation among students to be small and correspondingly reduce the correlation between mathematics aptitude and subtraction performance. In fact, if we set the mastery criterion at 100 percent and repeated the formative test-corrective instruction cycle until all students achieved this criterion, then the variance on the subtraction test would be zero, as would the correlation between aptitude and achievement.

However, this begs several critical questions. If some students take much longer than others to learn a particular objective, then one of two things must happen. Either corrective instruction must be given outside of the regular class time, or students who achieve mastery early on will have to waste considerable amounts of time waiting for their classmates to catch up. The first option, extra time, is expensive and difficult to arrange, as it requires that teachers be available outside of class time to work with the non-masters and that some students spend a great deal more time on any particular subject than they do ordinarily. The other option, putting rapid masters on hold with "enrichment" or "lateral extension" activities while corrective instruction is given, is unlikely to be beneficial for these students. For all students mastery learning poses a dilemma, a choice between content coverage and content master (see Arlin, 1984; Mueller, 1976; Resnick, 1977). It may often be the case that even for low achievers, spending the time to master each objective may be less productive than covering more objectives (see, for example, Cooley & Leinhardt, 1980).

PROBLEMS INHERENT TO MASTERY LEARNING RESEARCH

The nature of mastery learning theory and practice creates thorny problems for research on the achievement effects of mastery learning strategies. These problems fall into two principal categories: Unequal time and unequal objectives.

Unequal time. One of the fundamental propositions of mastery learning theory is that learning should be held constant and time should be allowed to vary, rather than the opposite situation held to exist in traditional instruction. However, if the total instructional time allocated to a particular subject is fixed, then a common level of learning for all students could only be achieved by taking time away from high achievers to increase it for low achievers, a leveling process that would in its extreme form be repugnant to most educators (see Arlin, 1982, 1984b; Arlin & Westbury, 1976; Fitzpatrick, 1985; Smith, 1981).

To avoid what Arlin (1984) calls a "Robin Hood" approach to time allocation in mastery learning, many applications of mastery learning provide corrective instruction during times other than regular class time, such as during lunch, recess, or after school (see Arlin, 1982). In short-term laboratory studies, the extra time given to students who need corrective instruction is often substantial. For example, Arlin & Webster (1983) conducted an experiment in which students studied a unit on sailing under mastery or non-mastery conditions for four days. After taking formative tests, mastery learning students who did not achieve a score of 80 percent received individual tutoring during times other than regular class time. Non-mastery students took the formative tests as final quizzes, and did not receive tutoring.

The mastery learning students achieved at twice the level of non-mastery students in terms of percent correct on daily chapter tests, an effect size of more than 3.0. However, mastery learning students spent more than twice as much time learning the same material. On a retention test taken four days after the last lesson, mastery students retained more than non-mastery students (effect size = .70). However, non-mastery students retained far more per hour of instruction than did mastery learning students (ES = -1.17).

In recent articles published in *Educational Leadership* and the *Educational Researcher,* Benjamin Bloom (1984a, b) noted that several dissertations done by his graduate students at the University of Chicago found effect sizes for mastery learning of one sigma or more (i.e., one standard deviation or more above the control group's mean). In all of these, corrective instruction was given outside of regular class time, increasing total instructional time beyond that allocated to the control groups. The additional time averaged 20-33 percent of the initial classroom instruction, or about one day per week. For example, in a two-week study in Malaysia by Nordin (1980) an extra period for corrective instruction was provided to the mastery learning classes, while control classes did other school work unrelated to the units involved in the study. A three-week study by Anania (1981) set aside one period each week for corrective instruction. In a study by Leyton (1983), students received 2-3 periods of corrective instruction for every 2-3 weeks of initial instruction. All of the University of Chicago dissertations cited by Bloom (1984 a. b) provided the mastery learning classes with similar amounts of additional instruction (Burke, 1983; Levin, 1979; Mevarech, 1980; Tenenbaum, 1982).

In discussing the practicality of mastery learning, Bloom (1984 a. p. 9) states that "...the time or other costs of the mastery learning procedures have usually been very small." It may be true that school districts could in theory provide tutors to administer corrective instruction outside of regular class time; the costs of doing so would hardly be "very small," but cost or cost-effectiveness is not at issue here. But as a question of experimental design, the extra time often given to mastery learning classes is a serious problem. It is virtually unheard-of in educational research outside of the mastery learning (method) to systematically provide an experimental group with more instructional time than a control group; presumably, any sensible instructional program would produce significantly greater achievement than a control method which involved 20-33 percent less instructional time.

It might be argued that mastery learning programs which provide corrective instruction outside of regular class time produce effects which are substantially greater per unit time than those associated with traditional instruction. However, computing "learning per unit time" is not a straight-forward process. In the Arlin and Webster (1983) experiment discussed earlier, mastery learning students passed about twice as many items on immediate chapter tests as did control students, and the time allocated to the mastery learning students was twice that allocated to control. Thus, the "learning per unit time" was about equal in both groups. Yet on a retention test only four days later, the items passed per unit time were considerably higher for the control group. Which is the correct measure of learning per unit time, that associated with the chapter tests or that associated with the retention test?

Many mastery learning theorists (e.g., Block, 1972; Bloom, 1976; Guskey, 1985) have argued that the "extra time" issue is not as problematic as it seems, because the time needed for corrective instruction should diminish over time. The theory behind this is that by ensuring that all students have mastered the prerequisite skills for each new unit, the need for corrective instruction on each successive unit should be reduced. A few brief experiments using specially constructed, hierarchically organized curriculum materials have demonstrated that over as many as three successive units, time needed for corrective instruction does in fact diminish (Anderson, 1976; Arlin, 1973; Block, 1972). However, Arlin (1984) examined time-to-mastery records for students involved in a mastery learning program over a four-year period. In the first grade, the ratio of average time to mastery for the slowest 25% of students to that for the fastest 25 percent was 2.5 to 1. Rather than decreasing, as would have been predicted by mastery learning theorists, this ratio increased over the four year period. By the fourth grade, the ratio was 4.2 to 1. Thus, while it is theoretically possible that mastery learning procedures may ultimately reduce the need for corrective instruction, no evidence from long-term practical applications of mastery learning supports this possibility at present.

It should be noted that many studies of mastery learning do hold total instruction time more or less constant across experimental and control conditions. In discussing the "best evidence" on practical applications of mastery learning, issues of time for corrective instruction will be explored further.

Utah Family Education Rights and Privacy Act

This appendix is included because many parents are appalled at the various kinds of non-academic testing their children have been subjected to but don't know what to do about it in their state. The following is the result of just such a group of parents in Utah who decided enough was enough and set out to pass a law that would make invasive testing of students illegal. They succeeded. So can you.

UTAH FAMILY EDUCATION RIGHTS AND PRIVACY ACT

An act relating to public education; requiring school personnel to comply with protection provided for family and student privacy; requiring school districts to enact policies to receive written parental permission prior to obtaining certain information from student relating to the student's family; and requiring advanced disclosure to parents.

Section 1. Section 53A-13-301, Utah Code Annotated 1953, is enacted to read:

Utah Family Education Rights and Privacy Act 53A-13-301. Application of federal law to administration and operation of public schools.

(1) Employees and agents of the state's public education system shall comply with the protection provided for family and student privacy under the Family Education Rights and Privacy Act, as enacted by United States Congress, in the administration and operation of all public school programs, regardless of the source of funding.

(2) Each public school district shall enact policies governing the protection of family and student privacy as required by this section.

Section 2. Section 53A-13-302, Utah Code Annotated 1953, is enacted to read:

53A-13-302. Prohibition of testing without prior written consent—Validity of consent—Qualifications.

Policies adopted by a school district under Section 53A-13-301 shall include prohibitions on:

(1) the administration of any psychological or psychiatric examination, test, or treatment, without prior written consent of the student's parent or legal guardian, in which the purpose of effect is to reveal information concerning the student's parent or legal guardian, in which the purpose or effect is to reveal information concerning the student's or any family member's:

(a) political affiliations or philosophies;

(b) mental or psychological problems;

(c) sexual behavior, orientation, or attitudes;

(d) illegal, anti-social, self incriminating, or demeaning behavior;

(e) critical appraisals of individuals with whom the student or family member has close family relationships;

(f) religious affiliations or beliefs;

(g) legally recognized privileged and analogous relationships, such as those with lawyers, medical personnel, or ministers; and

(h) income, except as required by law.

(2) The prohibitions regarding the inquiry or disclosing of information under Subsection (1) shall also apply to the curriculum or other school activities unless prior written consent of the student's parent or legal guardian has been obtained.

(3) Written parental consent is valid only if a parent or legal guardian has been first given written notice and a reasonable opportunity to obtain written information concerning:

(a) records or information, including information about relationships, that may be examined or requested;

(b) the means by which the records or information shall be examined or reviewed;

(c) the means by which the information is to be obtained;

(d) the purposes for which the records or information are needed;

(e) the entities or persons, regardless of affiliation, who will have access to the personally identifiable information; and

(f) a method by which a parent of a student can grant permission to access or examine the personally identifiable information.

(4) (a) Except in the case of exigent circumstances, disclosure to a parent or legal guardian must be given at least two weeks, but not more than five months before information protected under this section is sought.

(b) A general consent, including a general consent used to approve admission to or involvement in a special education or remedial program or regular school activity, does not constitute written consent under this section.

OBE Research Resources

1. "OBE SPECIAL": *An excellent resource to fight OBE.* A one-hour video on OBE produced by Channel 4 in Oklahoma City, Oklahoma. Video includes an interview with William Spady. Send check for $18 (including postage) to: Channel 4, P.O. Box 14068, Oklahoma City, OK 73113-0068.

2. Deliberate Dumb Down Packet (3-D Packet): More than five hundred pages of vital information to oppose restructuring efforts. Includes copies from educational journals and official government documents that prove current reforms (OBE/ML) are Skinnerian dumb-down, values-changing programs.

    Send $35 (including $4.95 priority postage) to Charlotte T. Iserbyt, 1062 Washington Street, Bath, ME 04530, or call 207-442-7899.

3. Mrs. C. Weatherly, Director of Education, Analysis, and Research Systems.

REPORT 1:   Analysis of H.R. 6 (reveals the complete change of the law) $5.00

REPORT 2:   The Real Meaning of "CHOICE" (analysis of government meaning of privatization) $1.25

Write to Director of Education, Analysis, and Research Systems, 1030 Sherwood Drive, Watkinsville, GA 30677, or call 706-769-7854.

4.   OBE—An Agenda With Many Names: Charlotte T. Iserbyt radio interviews on "Point of View" with Marlin Maddox. Two very interesting tapes (2679 and 2680) cover OBE and the history of U.S. government and tax-exempt foundation control of education in America. Call 800-347-5151 or write to "Point of View" Radio Talk Show, P.O. Box 30, Dallas, TX 75221 to order tapes.

5.   Pennsylvania Parent's Commission
P.O. Box 73
Johnstown, PA 15907
Peg Luksik

• Who Controls the Children? (video) $15.00
• Debate Tape (video) $18.00
• O.B.E. Documentation: A Primer ....$ 8.00
• 1992 Gamble-grams samples ....$ 5.00
• To Tell the Truth $10.00

Changing America's Form of Government With Patient Gradualism

Throughout the literature on outcome-based education we continually find references to representative democracy and participatory democracy. The more recent the material the more we find the term 'participatory.' Shirley McCune, director of the Mid-Continent Regional Education Laboratory (funded with federal tax dollars), declared at the Kansas Governors' Summit in 1989, "We are shifting from representative to participatory democracy." Oh really, Ms. McCune?

Apparently there are many things the education social interventionists intend to change in this country without telling the average American citizen. Add our form of government to the list.

Though the truth of the American form of government is rarely taught in any public school, Americans need to know the truth. We do not live under a democracy, contrary to what we have so often heard. We live under a republic. Remember "to the republic for which it stands, one nation under God." A review of Federalist Papers 10, 14, 48, and others, will reveal that the founders loathed the concept of democracy. This is precisely why they did not give us a government of a democracy but a form of a republic.

Article 4 section 4 of the U.S. Constitution guarantees the states a republican form of government. Nowhere is democracy identified. The founders understood a democracy to be nothing more than a fifty-one percent tyranny. In America personal rights are respected because the will of the fifty-one percent is bound by the restraints of the Constitution, the supreme law of our land.

A republic is a government of law and representation. A democracy inevitably becomes a mobocracy. What then is the agenda behind the OBE elite? McCune reveals that they are pressing for change—with patient gradualism. Why else would she say such things and the words "participatory democracy" appear in OBE handouts in states from Pennsylvania to Oregon? The more the concept of democracy is taught in our public schools, the less the value of our real form of government and the easier it is for government to act like a democracy and ultimately become a democracy. Patient gradualism is the method of those calling for the complete restructuring of society.

OBE
Quick Reference Guide

from Pam Hobbs Hoffecker,
writer education researcher

What is OBE, also known as "Education Reform," "Restructuring," and "Goals 2000"?

1. OBE (outcome-based education) is a marriage. The U.S. Department of Labor joined the U.S. Department of Education giving birth to "reinventing K-12 education" (*Learning A Living,* U.S. Department of Labor, 1992, xvi).

2. OBE is Skinnerian conditioning (behavior modification). Why? To create twenty-first century, politically correct, compliant laborers. How? The father of mastery learning, Benjamin Bloom, explains that the purpose of good teaching is to *change* a student's "thoughts, feelings and actions."

3. OBE challenges "fixed beliefs" (traditional family beliefs). A child must develop "higher cognitive levels of thinking" or "higher order thinking skills"—judging

problems in terms of *situations* rather than "fixed, dog-matic precepts" such as values clarification. (Bloom's *Taxonomy*, 55, 184).

4. OBE focuses on learning outcomes (goals), which are basically the same in each state. Over fifty percent of these outcomes (called "performance standards" in some states), are affective, that is, behavioral.

5. OBE creates data banks and electronic information systems. "WORKLINK will be an electronic information system linking local schools and employers" (*Learning A Living*, U.S. Department of Labor, 1992, 61). "Most Chinese live all their lives with files looming over them." The file is begun in school and "it shadows the person throughout life" (the *New York Times*, 26 March 1992). Ohio's data banks contain ninety-three categories on each student.

6. OBE uses assessment tests as the motor driving the whole OBE process. Ongoing assessment (assessing knowledge, thoughts, behaviors, and home life) of each student takes place about every four years. "How many magazines come into your house each week?" (Kansas form C4, 1992, 12.) "...Does your family get each month?" (Pennsylvania's PSAS, 1992, 2.)

7. OBE eliminates Carnegie Units (specific number of course credits required for graduation. "The Pennsylvania Federation of Teachers objects to the elimi-nation of courses required for graduation...dropping the Carnegie Unit" (Statement by the PaFT regarding... OBE). Instead, students must demonstrate with port-

folios, productions, and assessments that they have reached state outcomes. Achieving outcomes "may include extended days, weeks or years" (Kentucky, House Bill 940).

8. OBE eliminates school calendar mentality, increases the length of classes, and extends school year.

9. OBE requires unpaid community service for graduation. The Thirteenth Amendment to the Constitution states, "Neither slavery nor *involuntary* servitude, except as punishment for crime..."

10. OBE eliminates traditional graduation. Certificates of mastery of the outcomes, passports, and similar documents replace high school diplomas. (This has already been legislated in states such as Massachusetts, Oregon, and Washington.)

11. OBE also eliminates grades, initially in pre-kindergarten through third grade. Later grades (four through twelve) may blend as students learn in multi-aged groupings according to individual progress and remediation.

12. OBE requires teachers to become facilitator-coaches. Why? "Students must learn" (not teachers "teach"). Active learning (called twenty-first century "light learning" as opposed to twentieth century "paper training") necessitates cooperative learning, peer tutoring and, most importantly—extensive time on computers. [Indiana's Buddy System Project supplies a take-home computer ("buddy") to students.]

13. OBE requires site-based management. Rather than giving more local autonomy, building-based management will supersede *elected* school board control. Parent-councils at every school "take over much of the power wielded by local school boards" (the *Wall Street Journal,* 5 January 1993).

14. OBE requires partnerships. It's an octopus. OBE's tentacles include schools in partnership with businesses, health centers, career centers, youth centers, churches, and parents. Since parents are one of many tentacles— merely partners rather than owners—schools decide children's values and beliefs.

15. OBE is a dumbing-down process. Grades gradually inflate, while "tracking" (ability grouping), is eliminated. OBE reduces education to the lowest common denominator. School's focus shifts from academic to social engineering.

16. OBE requires state ownership of students. "We [Michigan's legislators] approved outcome-based education without seeing the full picture. The programming of little minds will take place..." (April 14, 1993, letter from Michigan State Senator Dinello adjuring Pennsylvania's legislators to vote *against* Pennsylvania's OBE bill).

Analysis of H.R. 6

This analysis of H.R. 6 is included because most people are totally unaware of what the federal government has done by changing the law. Right thinking people were outraged at the amendment to this bill that would have required *all* teachers in the U.S. to be certified. If passed into law this would have effectively eliminated all home schooling and compromised much private schooling as well. The outcry resonated from many parts of the country and the amendment went down in flames.

It was good to eliminate that dangerous clause, but what occurred while it was defeated was perhaps the most damaging change of all—sweeping changes and new powers for the federal government. The following analysis of H.R. 6 by Mrs. C. Weatherly, director of education, analysis, and research systems in Watkinsville, Georgia, outlines the most glaring of these changes and helps to put the bill into perspective.

UNION CALENDAR No. 325
103D CONGRESS
SECOND SESSION
H.R. 6

H.R. 6 is an omnibus bill originally presented to Congress in January 1993 as a reauthorization bill for the Elementary and Secondary Education Act of 1965. The first and last paragraphs of this 901-page tome are the only parts of the original bill which remain: 886 pages are printed in italics, which means that there are 886 pages of *new language*, otherwise known as new law.

Goals 2000 and the National Education Goals set forth by the National Education Goals Panel form the framework for H.R. 6. All of the education proposals in H.R. 6 are constructed in such a way as to cause "the Nation to meet the National Education Goals," as is so stated repeatedly throughout the bill. *Therefore, instead of a reauthorization bill for ESEA 1965, H.R. 6 becomes the implementation bill for Goals 2000 and the School-to-Work bills.*

There are some broad generalizations which can be made about the effects of H.R. 6. A few of them—but certainly not an exhaustive list—follow.

1. H.R. 6 provides for the restructuring of our country's education and social services delivery systems. These proposals can be found throughout the bill, from page 19 (c)(2) which states, "conditions outside the classroom such as hunger, unsafe living conditions, homelessness...can adversely affect children's academic achievement and *must be addressed through coordination of services, such as health and social services, in order for the Nation to meet the National Education*

Goals (emphasis added). (Editor's Note: Notice that the purpose for addressing the health and social issues is not to better living conditions for the children, but so that the "Nation" can "meet the National Education Goals.")

This wording and proposal reaches its zenith on page 323 which is the beginning of "Subpart 4—21st Century Community Learning Centers" under "Title II - Improving Teaching and Learning." Under Section 2441 Findings, "(1)...schools are in a unique position to identify student and family needs to coordinate programs;...(3) coordination of health and social service programs with education can help the Nation meet the National Education Goals and ensure better outcomes for children."

Under Section 2442 Funds for Community Learning Centers, "(a) In general, Local Education Agencies may use funds...to pay the Federal share...for enabling schools to serve as centers for the delivery of education and human services for members of the community."

The rest of this section, which ends on page 327, discusses the thirteen categories of services to be available— from literacy education programs, daycare, and parenting skills, to expected services for those who are "physically or mentally challenged." The terms "community education program," "merged or coordinated" programs, and "collaborative efforts" of agencies of a public nature *and* business are used repeatedly.

Also, beginning on Page 731, Title IX—General Provisions, and ending on page 751 there are continued references to consolidation of programs—both educational and otherwise—and consolidation of administrative procedures, grant applications, and reporting. The implications are that if a state or local education agency consolidates its programs, it may not have to account for the expenditure or administration of those funds or programs *separately*, but will report the overall effort and effect. This is commonly called "management by objective" (MBO), "planning, programming, budgeting, and evaluation" (PPBES), and "evidence of a controlled process."

These types of proposals give us cause to consider if perhaps our country's leadership has embraced a concept and philosophy of government quite foreign to that we've relied upon in the past.

2. Waiver of present law and practice are another repeated theme in this bill. There is an entire section on waivers, entitled "Part D—Waivers." On page 752, "Sec. 9401, Waivers of Statutory and Regulatory Requirements,: (a) General—...the Secretary may waive any requirement of this Act or of the General Education Provisions Act, or regulations issued under such Acts...if—(1) the Secretary determines that such requirement impedes the ability of State educational agency or other recipient to achieve more effectively the purposes of this Act...."

Let us remember that the purposes of this act center around meeting the National Education Goals. (Editor's Note: To be totally accurate I must include that there are exceptions to these broad waivers, but they are all centered on the issues of equity and civil rights provisions. Interestingly, though, they cannot suspend the regulation which allows a charter school to be free from state or local regulations as stated on page 348, Section 3407, Definitions. "(1)(A) in accordance with an enabling State Statute, is exempt from significant State or local rules that inhibit the flexible operation and management of public schools....")

3. The extent of the secretary's power to waive present federal practice granted under this bill is broad enough that it extends to at least *four* separate circumstances under which the prime contractor for a federal project is named. Usually federal contracts are let out for competitive bids and not named in enabling legislation. However, Reading Is Fundamental, Center for Civic Education, Kennedy Center for the Performing Arts, and Very Special Arts are specified as primary contractors in education programs and named in the bill itself. This is certainly a departure from established practice.

4. *Outcome-based education language and practices are scattered throughout H.R. 6.* The first mention of OBE language (identified from William Spady's High Success Network's training material and proposals) occurs on page 19: "All children can master challenging and complex problem-solving skills and research clearly shows that children...can succeed."

On page 20 there are continued references to OBE-related standards and practices including statements about how to evaluate what "children know and can do," receiving "supplemental help through extended-time activities" to meet the goals, and intensive attention to the acquisition of high-order-thinking skills. These themes occur throughout the bill with references to assessment and evaluation, "extended-time activities," extended school day, year, intensive staff development and retraining of teachers to meet the higher standards, and "transforming" teacher education.

On page 20 there are also references to "(6) the *disproven theory* that children must *learn basic skills before engaging in more complex tasks* continues to dominate strategies for classroom instruction, resulting in emphasis on repetitive drill and practice at the expense of content-rich instruction, accelerated curricula, and effective teaching to high standards" (emphasis added). This statement follows, "(4) use of *low-level tests* that are *not aligned with schools' curricula* fails to provide adequate information about what children know and can do and *encourages curricula and instruction that focus on the low-level skills* measured by such tests." This is absolutely fascinating because "low-level skills" *are* "basic skills" in educationese and "low-level tests" are norm-referenced tests which measure basic skills and concepts which are *indisputably* essential for children to be able to learn, think, and apply knowledge *independently.*

The fact that "low-level tests" are not "aligned to schools' curricula" gives us real insight into what is not being taught in our schools today! To teach complex tasks and "content-rich instruction" without a foundation of basic skills ensures *dependence* of the individual student upon constant reinforcement by teachers or others that they are mastering a task and removes any objective standard of achievement upon which students can build confidence in themselves and their abilities.

It also assures those who would program and channel our children into certain career paths beginning in grade six that all learning and achievement can be tailored to fit Spady's "orientations" for life roles, which means that students become dependent on the parameters of their learning because that is the only reinforcement of their ability available. *Limited learning for lifelong labor. Learning within context, not content.*

5. *Parents and parent skill training are mentioned alot in this bill.* Beginning on page 21, "(9) All parents *can* contribute

to their children's success by helping at home and *becoming partners with teachers* so that children can achieve high standards" (emphasis added).

On page 23 we find H.R. 6, "(6) affording parents meaningful opportunities to participate in the education of their children at home and at school...." Kind of them. Parenting skills are a part of those "consolidated services" provided by the 21st Century Community Learning Centers. Page 356 mentions arts education grants which will "(h) increase parental and community involvement in the educational, social, and cultural development of at-risk youth."

On page 80, under the Title I section, there begins a chapter which ends on page 88 describing the boundaries of parental involvement. This part states that agencies will receive funds if they implement "programs, activities, and procedures for the involvement of parents assisted under this title."

On page 83, (e) Shared Responsibilities for the High Student Performance, "each school served under this part shall jointly develop with parents for all children a school-parent compact that outlines how parents, the entire school staff, and students will share the responsibility for improved student achievement and the means by which the school and parents will build and develop a partnership....(1)... describe...the ways in which each parent will be responsible for supporting his or her children's learning, including monitoring attendance, homework completion, television watching, and positive use of extra-curricular time."

The rest of the section assures us that the parents will be trained to know how to do these activities and that community-based organizations and businesses will be enlisted to help. There will even be (on page 86) "(8)...[payment for] reasonable and necessary expenses associated with local parental involvement in activities including child care cost and transportation...to school-related meetings and training sessions...and (10) may train and support parents to enhance the involvement of other parents."

This whole process has been perfected in China, where they reinforce China's one-child policy through community education. It seems we are looking in strange places for our models of programs and to strange places (the federal government) for our nurturing. Mandated involvement with our children hardly comes from the heart and cannot be relied upon to sustain the activity, as demonstrated by the fact that this process has been tried before in the old Teacher Corps Community Councils of twenty years ago. If it had worked then, it would not be necessary to reintroduce it now.

The National Education Goals are demanding too much of us to offer so little in return. The development of an international, full-employment workforce will be difficult to draw upon in times of trouble when humanity and caring about each other have disappeared in the brilliant glow of global gold at the end of industry's rainbow.

6. *Speaking of "disappearing," the concept of our country's government and culture being conceived as a* constitutional republic *has no place in this bill.* On page 367, Part F, Civic Education, "Sec. 3701. Instruction on the History and Principles of Democracy in the United States." is found. On page 368, "(b)(1) a course of instruction on the basic principles of our constitutional *democracy* and the history of the Constitution and the Bill of Rights" (emphasis added) is first mentioned. This same wording is found in Section 3702 (b)(1)(b) on page 369 and is the same each time mentioned

thereafter. Such a slurring of the wording which describes our country's foundation should prepare us for the support for activities such as the community service requirement mentioned on page 370 (3).

These small signals, added to the overwhelming evidence of the thrust of H.R. 6 as a whole, should give us pause to consider that perhaps we will be embarking on a journey into new social and governmental territory.

Perhaps out response to H.R. 6 can be considered a national referendum on whether we are ready or willing to take the road to socialism. The constraints and contents of this bill certainly give us reason to consider this alternative.

7. *There are a few more nails yet to be hammered into the lid of whatever will contain the spread of H.R. 6.* Page 356 begins a section called "Community Arts." In this ten-page section we find some interesting statements:

(a) Findings—Congress finds that…

(2) the arts promote progress in academic subjects as shown by *research conducted by the National Endowment for the Arts* (Editor's Note: The National Endowment for the Arts is an objective research source?)….

(3) the arts *access multiple human intelligences* and develop higher order thinking skills (Editor's Note: The U.S. Department of Education certainly supports its grant recipients—Howard Gardner in this case. Do we wonder who is setting our educational agenda?)….

(4) the arts generate *self-esteem* and *positive emotional responses to learning* (Editor's Note: In what context? Is this when we use subliminal musical motivation as with Lazanov's *Super-Learning*?)…. (emphasis added, from page 354, section 3502).

(D) provide integration of community cultural resources in the regular curriculum...

(G) facilitate school-to-work transition from secondary schools and alternative schools to job training, higher education, and employment (page 355).

(D) to design collaborative cultural activities for students in secondary or alternative schools that ensure the smooth transition to job training, higher education, or *full employment* (Editor's Note: *Very* revealing wording in light of the other proposals in this bill. "Full employment" is part of Marxist economic theory).... (emphasis added, from page 359, under "Authorized Activities").

(J)...programs that use art *reform current school practices including lengthening the school day or academic year...*
Priority...the Secretary shall give priority to eligible entities that provide comprehensive services that extend beyond traditional school or service hour, that may provide year-round programs that provide services in the evenings and on weekends (Editor's Note: Federal coercion to make reforms that have been resisted locally).... (emphasis added, from page 360).

8. *Within this bill is an encouragement to pursue public school choice and the development of charter schools (which could be run by a non-profit organization or at least one that does not charge tuition.)* Under Title III, "Expanding Opportunities for Learning," there is much support for programs which meet and "contribute to the achievement of the National Education Goals" (page 327, Section 3201). The secretary is authorized to carry out such programs not only

through public entities, but also by *making grants* to or *contracting* with state, local, higher education agencies and "public and *private* agencies, organizations, and institutions" (emphasis added). The funds will support efforts that "promote *systemic educational reform*...such as:

(i) *research* and *development* related to content and performance standards...

(ii)...evaluation of *model strategies* for *assessment* of student learning, professional development for teachers and administrators, *parent and community involvement,* and other aspects of systemic reform (emphasis added).

The federal Department of Education is certainly involved in *every* aspect of this process. On page 329 the words "from preschool to school and from school to work... integration of education and health and social services..." again say it all.

There is much mentioned about evaluation and assessment, and page 330 includes the concept, "(L) experiential-based learning, such as service-learning" which takes in apprenticeships and community service.

Also on page 329 is a peculiar statement:

(D) activities to promote and evaluate counseling and mentoring for students including *intergenerational mentoring* (emphasis added).

While "mentoring" is clearly understood and in fact is defined on page 736 as meaning "a program in which an adult works with a child or youth on a 1-to-1 basis," the interjection of the additional wording on page 329, "inter-generational," immediately throws a different light on the intent of this section. Granted, not everyone is fully acquainted with the language variances of the pedophile movement, but those who are recognize this emphasis as one which comes from that sector. This should give pause about the authorship and intent of this paragraph in H.R. 6.

9. *The comprehensiveness of any type of involvement with H.R. 6 and the National Education Goals should cause private schools who have availed themselves of federal program grants to local systems in the past to pause.* This bill makes it abundantly clear that the government wants *everyone* trained the same way. The handwriting should be on the wall about the dangers in this climate of receiving any public support (such as vouchers and tax credits) for private or homeschooling.

10. *Page 898 contains a detailed outline of how the Secretary will conduct a* comprehensive *study of how well everyone has been assisted to "reform their educational systems through the various education laws enacted by the 103rd Congress" (see Title V, "Miscellaneous").*

If you would like more information about H.R. 6, call or write

DIRECTOR OF EDUCATION, ANALYSIS AND SYSTEMS,
MRS. C. WEATHERLY
1030 SHERWOOD DR.
WATKINSVILLE, GA 30677
706-769-7854

The Swedish Model

For decades Sweden was the premier welfare state. Progressives touted its smorgasbord of subsidies that ranged from government-run day care to nearly unlimited sick leave. But to pay for all that Sweden imposed taxes that at one point consumed 56 percent of the nation's output. The Swedish people, saddled with inefficient monopoly services and two decades of low growth, finally voted the Socialists out of power last fall.

Carl Bildt, Sweden's new 42-year-old conservative prime minister, aims to steer Sweden back into the family of free-market nations. "Collectivism and socialism have been thrown on the scrap heap of history," he told us during a recent visit. "There is no compromise worth having between state control and capitalism."

After only six months in power, Mr. Bildt has already abolished taxes on wealth and inheritance, cut government spending by two percent in real terms, and begun an aggressive privatization program. Services from medicine to child care are being opened up to private competition.

But nowhere is the break with the past as sharp as it is in education. Swedish schools have been touted as the most "progressive" in the world, relentlessly pursuing equality at the expense of excellence. Grades were abolished for students under the age of 15, because they were said to foster competition rather than cooperation among students.

All that is changing under the instruction of Beatrice Ask, Sweden's new 35-year-old education minister. She says that although Sweden spends $7,000 a year per student on education—more than any other country—its young people have only middling scores on comparative international tests and are slipping.

Ms. Ask has a bold reform agenda which begins with reintroducing grades, requiring that English be taught from the first grade on and encouraging the study of Christian ethics in schools.

Ms. Ask says Americans should think carefully before they follow Sweden's former example and view schools as a center for the delivery of social services. "Swedish schools have diluted the quality of education by trying to do too much," she says. "They may then neglect their basic function—educating children."

The government will also end the state's virtual monopoly on education. Government education money will go to individual students instead of schools, allowing parents the freedom to send their children to any private or public school. "Free competition will provide better value for the money spent, increase the role of parents in education and lead to more innovation," says Ms. Ask. She is a fan of Poland's educational reforms, which include a voucher program to encourage the formation of a private-school sector.

After being praised for six decades for supposedly finding a "Third Way" between socialism and capitalism, Sweden's new leaders are amused that their bold reforms aren't getting more attention in the West. "Now that we have decided the Third Way is actually a blind alley, we had hoped the world would want to learn from our pioneering example," says Finance Minister Bo Lundgren.

Indeed, Sweden's experience with collectivism and the nanny-state contains valuable lessons for those American liberals who continue to oppose educational choice and promote industrial policy and centralized health care. Perhaps some foundation should fly a few of them over to Stockholm so they can learn from the New Swedish Model.